LOWELL L. BENNION

Introductions to Mormon Thought

Edited by Matthew Bowman and Joseph Spencer
A list of books in the series appears at the end of this book.

LOWELL L. BENNION

A Mormon Educator

GEORGE B. HANDLEY

UNIVERSITY OF
ILLINOIS PRESS
Urbana, Chicago, and Springfield

Library of Congress Cataloging-in-Publication Data
Names: Handley, George B., 1964– author.
Title: Lowell L. Bennion : a Mormon educator / George B.
    Handley.
Description: Urbana : University of Illinois Press, [2023]
    | Series: Introductions to Mormon thought | Includes
    bibliographical references and index.
Identifiers: LCCN 2023001879 (print) | LCCN 2023001880
    (ebook) | ISBN 9780252045394 (cloth) | ISBN
    9780252087516 (paperback) | ISBN 9780252054990
    (ebook)
Subjects: LCSH: Bennion, Lowell L., 1908–1996. | College
    teachers—Utah—Biography. | Mormon authors—Utah—
    Biography. | Church of Jesus Christ of Latter-day Saints—
    Doctrines.
Classification: LCC LA2317.B376 H36 2023 (print) |
    LCC LA2317.B376 (ebook) | DDC 289.3/32092 [B]—
    dc23/eng/20230125
LC record available at https://lccn.loc.gov/2023001879
LC ebook record available at https://lccn.loc.gov/2023001880

For Lindsay, Brian, and John

Contents

Foreword to the
Introductions to Mormon Thought Series   ix
  Matthew Bowman and Joseph Spencer

Acknowledgments   xi

CHAPTER ONE
The Life of a Mormon Educator   1

CHAPTER TWO
The Abundant Life   33

CHAPTER THREE
A Rational Faith   55

CHAPTER FOUR
Social Morality   78

Bibliographic Essay   105

Notes   113

Works Cited   117

Index   121

Foreword to the Introductions
to Mormon Thought Series

Our purpose in this series is to provide readers with accessible and short introductions to important figures in the intellectual life of the religious movement that traces its origins to the prophetic career of Joseph Smith, Jr. With an eye to the many branches of that movement (rather than solely to its largest branch, the Church of Jesus Christ of Latter-day Saints), the series gathers studies of what scholars have long called *Mormon* thought. We define "thought" and "intellectual life," however, quite as broadly as we define "Mormonism." We understand these terms to be inclusive, not simply of formal theological or scholarly work, but also of artistic production, devotional writing, institutional influence, political activism, and other non-scholarly pursuits. In short, volumes in the series assess the contributions of men and women who have shaped how those called Mormons in various traditions think about what "Mormonism" is.

We hope that this series marks something of a coming of age of scholarship on this religious tradition. For many years, Mormon studies have focused primarily on historical questions largely of internal interest to the (specifically) Latter-day Saint community. Such historical work has also mainly addressed the nineteenth century. Scholars have accordingly established the key sources for the study of Mormon history and culture, and they have established a broad consensus on many issues surrounding the origins and character of the religious movement. Recent work, however, has pushed academics into the work of comparison, asking larger questions in two key ways. First, recent scholars have approached these topics from a greater variety of disciplines. There has emerged in Mormon studies, in other words, increasing visibility for the disciplines of philosophy, sociology, literary criticism, and media studies, among others. Second, scholars working this field have also begun to consider new topics of study—in particular gender and sexuality, the status of international Mormonism, and the experience of minority groups within the tradition. We believe the field has thus reached the point where the sort of syntheses these books offer is both possible and needed.

Given these commitments, George Handley's work on Lowell Bennion is an obvious addition to the series. Active from the 1930s to the 1990s, Bennion was one of the most influential Latter-day Saint thinkers of the twentieth century. In many ways, he is the grandfather of modern Mormon liberalism. It was a term he embraced. His emphasis on religion as preeminently about practice rather than about doctrinal orthodoxy, his belief that the preeminent aim of religion should be the achievement of a just and righteous community on earth, and his focus on education as the primary means of conveying religious values all mark him not only as a transformative figure in the Latter-day Saint movement, but as a quintessential early twentieth-century American religious liberal. All of these characteristics were shared widely among Protestant, Catholic, and Jewish religious liberals, and Bennion is thus of interest not simply as a Mormon figure, but as an illustration of the ecumenism of the movement. Like many other American religious liberals, he was steeped in European Christian thought. Indeed, he was the author of one of the earliest English-language studies of the work of German sociologist Max Weber. But he was also committed to the tangible, hands-on work of cultivating religious virtue, known for his love of farming and his commitment to personal service. His mixture of philosophical sophistication and homespun community building marks him, then, not only as a religious liberal, but a quintessential Mormon.

Matthew Bowman
Joseph Spencer

Acknowledgments

Scholarship is an ongoing dialogue with forebears and peers on behalf of those still to come. As such, despite the many hours one spends alone in producing it, it is a collaborative venture. My work here is a dialogue with the thought of one forebear, Lowell L. Bennion, and also with many colleagues and friends who believe in the high ideals of religious education that inspired Bennion and in the loving criticism he so ably embodied.

My debt to Lowell Bennion is considerable. I was fortunate to have had the experience of attending his boys ranch in Victor, Idaho, as a young boy in the late 1970s and then as a camp counselor as a very green, not-quite-adult in the summers of 1983 and 1984. In the stunning environment of Teton Valley, I learned at his side, and my life continues to reap the benefits. Before I was old enough to appreciate the significance of his generosity, he befriended my schizophrenic uncle, took him to Europe with his family, and gave him opportunities to be of service. I devoured his books in the years that followed, recognizing in them many of the teachings he had shared with us over those unforgettable summer months. This brought me into lifelong and stimulating dialogue with fellow Latter-day Saints who shared Bennion's belief in the value of education, his loyalty to the religious life, and his commitment to service.

These fruits of his influence are a chief reason I have chosen to teach at Brigham Young University for the past twenty-five years and why my years there have been an adventure of a lifetime. Even though my reader will note that, at times, as I assess the heights of Bennion's thought, I find religious education and culture in the Latter-day Saints (LDS) context wanting, I have benefited greatly from the very real achievements of the venture of religious education and remain a firm believer in the project. I offer this analysis in the hope that it will help to keep the trajectory positive. I offer it too in the spirit of these words of Lowell: "I have confidence inspired by decades of public discourse that, if both of us will keep talking and keep listening, the results will please us both. It is impatience with another's point of view, an insistence on immediate action, the exercise of power before that process of dialogue occurs, or imposition of a policy without willingness to explain, listen, patiently explain again that I mistrust" (1988a, vi).

I am grateful to early readers of this manuscript who have provided excellent advice on it, including Terryl Givens, Phil Barlow, Ryan Davis, Steve Peck, Morgan Davis, Fred Axelgard, Bill Turnbull, and Thomas McConkie. I presented overviews of the book to colleagues at the Maxwell Institute, the Mormon History Association, and Mormon Scholars in the Humanities, where I received both needed encouragement and valuable suggestions. Abby Pinegar was an outstanding research assistant on this project. And, finally, series editors Matt Bowman and Joe Spencer were extraordinary, Alison Syring Bassford at the University of Illinois Press has been very supportive, and Jack Newell and an anonymous reader at University of Illinois Press gave substantive and thorough editorial guidance. I was also fortunate to consult with and receive encouragement from two of Lowell's children, Steven and Ben, and his grandson, Lindsay. Despite the rich dialogue I have enjoyed on the topics that Bennion addressed in his writings and on Bennion's invaluable insights in particular, I accept responsibility for the interpretations and assessments my reader will find in these pages.

LOWELL L. BENNION

CHAPTER ONE

The Life of a Mormon Educator

Lowell L. Bennion (1908–1996) is certainly among the greatest humanitarians to emerge from the Church of Jesus Christ of Latter-day Saints. His life was a masterful sermon and exemplum of Latter-day Saint values. Bennion began introducing his students to hands-on service opportunities in his role as director of the LDS Institute at the University of Utah in the 1940s, a tradition that was later commemorated by the creation of the Lowell Bennion Community Service Center at the University of Utah in 1987. The center continues to flourish, bringing hundreds of students every year into the community and successfully integrating service to the disadvantaged into the curricular experience of the university. Bennion also founded a boys' ranch in the 1960s that focused on work and service and that operated for more than two decades, becoming the model for camps for boys and girls in various locations. From 1972 to 1988, he was director of the Community Service Council in Salt Lake City, where he facilitated coordination between civic leaders and nonprofit organizations and directed countless projects aimed at helping the elderly, the mentally ill, the physically handicapped, and the homeless and destitute. In addition, he was a lifelong champion and hands-on worker for racial integration and justice. Christian service, in short, was not a theory or merely a value for Lowell Bennion. It was a way of life. If this were a book only about his life, its subtitle would have to be "A Mormon Humanitarian."

This is a book, however, chiefly dedicated to Bennion's thought, and he was as masterful a thinker and educator as he was a humanitarian. Although he wasn't inclined to identify himself as such, he was among the most important LDS theologians of the twentieth century and certainly its foremost ethicist. He stands perhaps alone in history as the only non-General Authority of the Church of Jesus Christ of Latter-day Saints to have spoken not once, but twice in General Conference, offering advice on education and on courtship and marriage. In well-crafted manuals that he wrote for the LDS Church for almost thirty years and in his own much beloved small books that he published in the years after his institutional career ended in 1962, he offered a remarkably consistent and coherent articulation of the grounds for Christian belief and Christian living in the modern world. Trained as a sociologist with a keen and detached understanding of the complexities of religious institutions and of contemporary life and thought, he was also a devout believer committed to helping the LDS Church and its members minimize the risks of the religious life and realize its fullest potential. As a religious educator, in other words, he was both a living example and an intellectual guide for an adventurous life of faith in the modern world.

The integrity he lived was modeled in his thought, and this made Bennion a deceptively simple thinker. He advocated a life of "simple living and high thinking," but even his high thinking was offered in prose accessible to any reader (Bennion 1996, 91). This is because, as he wisely put it, "Abstract theology has its place, but it saves no one either in this life or in eternity." Ideas and beliefs, if they were ever to have any power to shape life meaningfully, needed to become "real and internalized" in the lives of readers (Bennion 1983, vii). The value of thought, in other words, was measured by its capacity to provide the ethical grounds and motivations to improve life. The ethical focus of his thought, guided by the fundamental teachings of Christ and of the Old Testament prophets, allowed him to search new social, scientific, and political realities without resorting to esotericism. In close to sixty years of writing, he modeled how Mormonism could thrive in the modern world by translating modern life and lived experience into commonsense spiritual understanding with exceptional skill, thereby strengthening *and expanding* fundamental Latter-day Saint ideas and values.

In his 1957 landmark study published with the University of Chicago Press, *The Mormons*, sociologist Thomas O'Dea had correctly identified a tension in the modern Latter-day Saints church between its push toward education and its pull toward its supernatural claims, a tension he openly worried tended toward a self-destructive anti-intellectual protectionism. In reference to one unnamed institute director with whom he spoke, O'Dea identified one possible way forward. From his summary, we can deduce with some confidence that the man in question was Bennion himself:

> One man who was unusually perceptive in that regard did talk to me about the vast potentialities for development that he saw in Mormon theology because of the great variety of its doctrinal sources. . . . It was possible, he continued, to draw on these and develop what was best in them, laying special emphasis upon what was best in the teachings of the prophets and Christ. He emphasized the importance of the belief in a personal God who communicated with men—"a living God"—and in the personal immortality of man. He especially stressed the centrality of Christ and the importance of reorienting Mormon teachings with respect to present-day problems on the basis of the teachings of Christ. (O'Dea 1957, 238)

Bennion's books offered Mormonism a way to understand and be truer to itself as it emerged from isolation and obscurity. In the end, he was loved as much for his service as for his role as a teacher, in part for the same reason: his life and thought were consistent with each other and consistently and deeply Christian. In sum, he is also arguably the most influential Latter-day Saint educator of the past century.

Philip Barlow once called Bennion Mormonism's "great communicator" and insisted that he would be remembered more for his books than because of his teaching and service (Bradford 1995, 344). Eugene England called him "Mormonism's greatest practical philosopher" (England, 1996, 29). And yet now, with twenty-five years of hindsight since his death, he is hardly remembered at all. Younger Latter-day Saints know nothing of him, church leaders do not cite him, and his books have long been out of print. The neglect could be explained by the natural decline of popularity that comes with time and by a growing and increasingly international church, but there are other authors of his time—Hugh Nibley comes to mind—that remain at least reasonably well known today. One might expect too that perhaps his independent books written in the later years of his life manifested new levels of boldness or of criticism that might have caused some disfavor. Remarkably, however, one cannot find any significant shift in tone, themes, or reasoning in his writing between the very first edition of his first manual he wrote for the LDS Church in 1939, *The Religion of the Latter-day Saints*, and his posthumous book of 1996, *How Can I Help?*

I submit that, if there was a change, it was in the institutional and cultural matrix that surrounded him. After the 1960s, the Church of Jesus Christ of Latter-day Saints no longer produced manuals written by individual authors but instead produced them by committee, a process known as correlation. This created a more uniform, impersonal, and stripped-down approach that intended to minimize variation across religious instruction in Sunday worship, in institutes and seminaries for college and high school students, and to a degree in religious education at church-owned universities such as Brigham Young University. While this seemingly benign shift in institutional practice proved effective in creating more uniformity in church life across an increasingly international church, it implicitly squelched the creativity of interpretation and application of religious belief to the whole of one's life that Bennion had long insisted was the chief prerogative and opportunity of the Christian faithful. Bennion's approach to religious education emphasized the goal of finding harmony between the ontological claims of religion with secular learning and the contemporary secular circumstances of life. His was a practical and ethical view of religion that sought to empower believers to do God's work in their particular circumstances. Bennion was a firm believer in the doctrines of his church, but he believed that their value was not merely salvific in the world to come but that they had power here and now to change lives for the better. Correlated manuals, by contrast, tended to focus on the cultivation of individual belief, placing a premium on salvation and on "testimony" or a personal witness of spiritual truths, leaving the larger intellectual, political, and cultural circumstances of life unaddressed. The implication of correlation, even if it was unintended, was that doctrine was either at odds with lived experience and rigorous analysis or irrelevant. This had been O'Dea's worry; if doctrinal claims appeared to be in an indifferent or even antagonistic posture toward the intellectual and experiential realms of life, the LDS Church would struggle to keep its youth engaged and to promote among all members a thoughtful and principled engagement with the secular world.

It would be consistent with O'Dea's unnamed source to identify three main themes in Bennion's writings as a roadmap for a thriving LDS faith in the modern world; they are the focus of the subsequent three chapters in this book. First, he believed that collectively Old Testament prophetic wisdom, New Testament teachings of Jesus Christ, and latter-day scriptures and revelations all prioritized the full flourishing of individuals endowed with divine and eternal potential, here and now. This Latter-day Saint value placed on the individual, he hoped, would inspire individuals to pursue the abundant life and would protect them against the dehumanizing tendencies of dogmatism, authoritarianism, and ennui that can emerge in institutional contexts. Second, he insisted on a rational faith, one in which revelation and continual learning of all kinds were both necessary. Religious education should not be compartmentalized but fully integrated into the life experience and education of a Latter-day Saint. And, finally, he promoted what he called social morality as a vital form of Christian discipleship in contemporary life. There was no sense in cherishing beliefs if they didn't translate into ethical commitments and meaningful transformation of character and society.

Three brief anecdotes from his life might suffice to exemplify the themes of an abundant life, a rational faith, and social morality and to suggest some of the institutional tensions that he would encounter. Sometime in 1956 or 1957, Lowell became aware of a white student who had learned of his African ancestry, which prevented him from participation in the priesthood ordinances and had led church leaders to prevent his sister's temple sealing. Lowell took the case straight to his mentor, President David O. McKay. In his interview with McKay, he pleaded, "President McKay, in my experience, the gospel builds life. Here I see it tearing it down." McKay explained that he had discontinued a practice of requiring a certification of genealogical purity in South Africa in the face of such conundrums. Clearly troubled by the priesthood ban and the administrative burdens it placed on his shoulders, McKay confided, "When problems like this come to be, I say to myself, 'Sometime I shall meet my Father in Heaven, and what will he say?'" Bennion offered his own answer: "He'll forgive you if you err on the side of mercy." McKay was persuaded and allowed the young woman's temple sealing (Bradford 1995, 165–66). Bennion understood that institutions would always have to balance consideration of individual lives with their own institutional self-interest unless they were willing to fail to build life.

Not long after Apostle John Widstoe had hired the young Bennion to direct the LDS Institute at the University of Utah in 1935, he bumped into Bennion in a bookstore, grabbed him by the lapel, and asked, "Brother Bennion, do you still believe the gospel is true?" Bennion retorted, "Elder

Widstoe, as far as it's interpreted correctly" (Bennion 1985b, 84). This anecdote captures both the intimacy and humor of their friendship and Bennion's awareness of the ironically wide range of interpretation that was inherently at play in church life. The gospel that believers purported to believe in, in other words, wasn't always the same thing as the gospel truth. For Bennion, refinement, circumspection, education, and ongoing revelation were vital to healthy and vibrant belief in religious life, even if that meant that conformity would be harder to come by. Bennion felt, again, that balance was not only possible but necessary.

A third and final anecdote is from 1938, when J. Reuben Clark, then a member of the First Presidency, issued an address to church educators, *The Charted Course of the Church in Education*, in which he denounced the modernist emphasis on ethics and briefly articulated the fundamental doctrinal claims of the Restored Gospel. He asserted that "The tithing represents too much toil, too much self-denial, too much sacrifice, too much faith, to be used for the colorless instruction of the youth of the Church in elementary ethics" (Clark 1938, 11). Many LDS educators were disturbed by the talk, and some resigned in protest. M. Lynn Bennion, Lowell's brother, who was then serving as supervisor of LDS seminaries, called it "alarming" (Simpson 2016, 120). Bennion's response is instructive. A year later, he published his first manual for the LDS Church in which he tied the doctrines Clark proclaimed to ethics. He did so, however, without fanfare or direct contradiction. He simply put his faith in the reasoning behind his interpretations of scripture. In a chapter that develops an understanding of the law of consecration, for example, Bennion tells his reader, "The student will recognize this religious interest in the socio-economic interest of the gospel of Jesus Christ in the lives of men. If 'men are that they might have joy,' then religion must penetrate and influence the most vital experiences of men. Gaining a livelihood is certainly one of these. Community life is another, maintaining health still another" (1940, 189). For Bennion, Christ's gospel didn't offer a choice between supernatural beliefs about the life to come and a focus on the temporal circumstances of humanity, as Clark had implied, but a marriage of earth and heaven: "religion must grapple with life here and now in order to prepare man for heavenly things" (1940, 187). Latter-day Saint teachings, as he saw them, shouldn't force choices between reason and faith, belief and ethics, or between a spiritual and a temporal focus.

Despite the remarkable consistency and power of his ideas, Bennion's lifelong loyalty to the LDS Church, and the high esteem in which he was held throughout his life, Bennion moved from being an official and employed voice of authority on such questions to an increasingly neglected writer whose audience has narrowed over time. This was especially true as the LDS Church sought consolidation in the context of its rapid growth. Although his manuals and books were offered in the spirit of defending his church's relevance and importance in the modern world and were often received as such, they were met early with some ambivalence among the LDS hierarchy, an ambivalence that persisted to the end of his life.

One important factor especially contributed to the ambivalence. Starting at the time of Brigham Young, the Church of Jesus Christ of Latter-day Saints had banned men of African descent from holding the priesthood, and this policy became increasingly controversial during the civil rights era and even long after it was overturned in 1978. In the 1930s, when Bennion's career began, Mormonism needed and eagerly welcomed articulations of its unique and special place in the modern world, and he gladly complied. By the time of the civil rights era, however, it had become increasingly clear that his teachings about the dignity of individuals, the contingency of revelation, and social morality implicitly argued against the ban and the various justifications for it. It was never his intention to embarrass or hurt his church, but he also refused to remain silent when justifications for the ban were offered. Indeed, his loving criticism on this issue, despite its consistently measured and moderate tone, was a key reason why he was ultimately dropped from church employment and his institutional influence waned. Bennion had offered a path for the faithful to understand with humility the reality of both individual and institutional error and to labor faithfully in hope of what he saw as the LDS Church's divine call to ennoble all human souls. As US society grew increasingly intolerant of the LDS Church policy, however, church leaders either remained silent or defensive, making an acknowledgment of racism harder. Although the ban was reversed in a revelation to President Spencer W. Kimball in 1978, no explanation for the ban or admission of error was offered, and even up to Bennion's death in 1996, no further institutional action was taken to redress racism.

Of course, Bennion would have been pleased to hear his former neighbor and friend, Gordon B. Hinckley, who became President of the Church of

Jesus Christ of Latter-day Saints in 1995 just before Bennion died, denounce racism in 2006. He would similarly have welcomed the LDS Church's publication of the Gospel Topics Essay in 2013 on race and the priesthood that disavowed the various theories that justified the ban and acknowledged past racism. He would have celebrated President Russell M. Nelson's friendship and collaboration with the NAACP that began in 2019. Bennion had personally worked on these fronts decades before without apology, fanfare, or defensiveness. Sadly, he didn't live to see these institutional events transpire, which arguably represented the direction he desired his church to take.

As the LDS Church continues to struggle to fully confront legacies of discrimination and to make satisfactory room—both theologically and institutionally—for differences of race, gender, and sexuality in the contemporary church, Bennion remains an untapped resource. In an age of increasing anxiety, decreasing trust in institutions, rampant consumerism, and political tribalism, his call to center institutional practice on human dignity, to promote the integration of faith and reason, and to inspire humble living and consecrated commitment to social morality would be a welcome help.

A Biography

By all accounts, Bennion's childhood with his parents, Milton and Cora, and his siblings was full of loving attention and creativity and was characterized by a liberal spirit of trust, tolerance, and freedom in decision making. As the fifth of ten children, he was born in 1908 in Forest Dale, an area near what is today known as Sugar House in Salt Lake City, Utah. Lowell described his family circumstances in this way: "I was really blessed with great pride in my heritage and my uncles and aunts and grandparents, and very blessed with my father and mother, their character and attitudes. And I had a vigorous, stimulating life with my brothers and sisters. We weren't passive in any sense" (Bennion 1985b, 32).

Lowell was a direct beneficiary of the Latter-day Saint emphasis on self-development and education. Milton (1870–1953), named in honor of the English poet, became an educator of great capacity who motivated several generations of educators. After obtaining an MA from Columbia University, Milton started teaching pedagogy at the University of Utah in 1901 and was later appointed dean of education in 1913, when Lowell was only five, in which capacity he served until 1941. He also served on the LDS Church's Sunday School board for forty years, including stints as assistant and general superintendent. Lowell remembers an ethical focus in his father's teachings and a strong respect for his children's agency, drawing frequently from Proverbs, the Psalms, and the New Testament (Bradford 1995, 17). Toward the end of his life, Bennion confirmed that his faith, career, and "my ethics and my values" were indelibly shaped by Milton's example as a believing and humble intellectual who gave his gifts to the quest for social improvement of others (Bennion 1985b, 27).

In 1919, Milton published a scholarly work, *Citizenship: An Introduction to Social Ethics* with a New York publisher, and *Moral Teachings of the New Testament* with Deseret Book in 1928 for members of his church. In both cases, he laid out an argument for ethics as an indispensable dimension to the religious life. He was an active voice in the educational controversies of his day, working to protect academic freedom (including coming to the defense of educators under fire for teaching evolution) while also urging a moral purpose to education and a harmonious partnership with his own Latter-day Saint tradition. A man of great humility, Milton was also an important intellectual influence in Utah, comfortable and familiar with church and civic leaders alike. His friendship with high-level church leaders modeled for young Lowell a way of interacting with them that wouldn't compromise his own integrity or his ability to express his own opinion in public and in print.

Lowell showed academic promise early, skipping two grades and graduating from high school at the age of fifteen and starting classes at the University of Utah. One important influence at the university, Arthur Beeley, provided a crucial catalyst for Lowell's growing interest in the prospects for a life of the mind. Beeley was among a wave of Latter-day Saint professors who earned their degrees at elite institutions of the east—in his case in social science at the University of Chicago—and who returned to Utah with a passionate determination to integrate faith and intellectual inquiry within the Latter-day Saint community. Beeley inspired the young Bennion with talk of a "renaissance of Mormonism" that he believed could come from the application of social science to the problems of the LDS Church (Bennion 1985b, 44).

Lowell found a compatible intellectual and spiritual companion in Merle Colton, whom he had met in their ward in Forest Dale sometime after 1924.

Merle and Lowell married in 1928, only for Lowell to depart to the Swiss-German mission six weeks later. As the proverb says, the distance only increased their fondness for one another, as they spent the next 2½ years in affectionate correspondence while he developed and shared his love of the German language and the people of his mission. His father persuaded him to stay in Europe when his mission was complete to pursue his education and offered some modest financing for him to begin classes at the University of Erlangen in Nürnberg in 1931. To begin this new phase of his life, he was finally reunited with his beloved Merle, who moved to Europe to join him.

Germany, of course, was on the cusp of historic change, change that even the astute budding scholar didn't initially perceive. At one point, out of intellectual curiosity, Bennion attended a pro-Nazi rally and later expressed regret that he did not sense "more keenly than I did where it would all lead" (Bradford 1995, 46). It was disturbing enough, however, to convince him to transfer to the University of Vienna, where he witnessed further civil unrest. Now more aware of what the changes portended, at one point, he and a friend escorted a fellow Jewish student to protect him from a raucous crowd. Despite the signs of increasing intolerance, Merle and Lowell enjoyed a brief idyll in their multicultural branch of various European immigrants, and the university provided a haven where Lowell was formally introduced to sociology and to the thought of Max Weber, whom he described as "the most creative, expansive mind I ever met" (Bradford 1995, 48). Rising anti-Semitism and demonstrations made the young couple increasingly uneasy, and so they eventually transferred again, this time to France, to the University of Strasbourg, where he completed the very first English-language study of Weber in 1933.

Weber suggested to Bennion reasons to worry about the risks and challenges of bureaucratization, what Weber described as the rationalization of culture, but also the ways in which values and ideals can be used creatively to mitigate those risks and achieve real and beneficial social results. Weber rejected the reductionism and determinism of much Marxist thought that tended to see culture, including religion, as a by-product of underlying economic conditions. He worried, however, that all systems of knowledge, including religion itself and academic disciplines, tended to become autonomous and answerable only to themselves, a move that fueled their competitive ascendancy but also limited the capacity of either to respond to lived experience. Weber had shown that, as Christianity became detached from broader society and experience and became a more private matter, its values had given rise to the practices and spirit of modern capitalism. Although Weber was harshly critical of that spirit of accumulation, a spirit that had resulted in what he famously described as contemporary culture's "iron cage" of bureaucratic rule, Bennion saw Weber as also suggesting that a potential solution to such problems lay in their very causes. That is to say, values, including religious values, might help to mitigate the very conditions that they had once helped to create, if they could be rediscovered as such, instead of as merely institutional norms, and more deliberately and self-consciously redirected for better ends. Weber inductively derived what he called ideal types from historical and cultural contexts and then used them to make comparative judgments of systems across cultures. This method suggested to Bennion the vital role religion could play in shaping institutions and cultures, as long as the academic disciplines and religious values could remain engaged in a mutual commitment to escape their iron cages by learning together how to better serve the whole of the human experience. In short, Bennion saw hope in Weber's respect for the irreducibility of the inner human life and the power of values to shape the conditions of life.

Weber distinguished value judgments from factual propositions, a distinction that Bennion felt gave room for religion and secular learning in the development of the whole person and of the whole society (Bennion 1985b, 80–81). Of different epistemologies, he said, "You can be a politician and a scientist, but you have to know what you are at any one time. You have to shift gears and know you are shifting. That's the thing I learned from Max Weber" (Bennion 1985b, 75). Building on the inspiration Beeley gave him, Bennion sensed Weber's methodology could help improve his church's ability to allow human personalities to flourish. During five years in Europe as a missionary and as a student, he had learned to apply his values to working to improve the society that he was in, as well as to set aside values and religious interest enough to understand and learn from empirical reality.

In short, Weber gave Bennion a way to understand the power of his own Latter-day Saint theology in a modern context and to understand the rationalization and bureaucratization of his own culture that his father had observed up close and that would soon become his own professional context for the next six decades. Bennion never seems to have wavered in his own convictions about the truth of revelation as proclaimed by the Latter-day Saint faith, but he was animated by the prospect of understanding his Latter-day Saint experience in a scientific light and contributing in new and original ways to the challenges that lay before the LDS Church in its efforts to realize its educational ambitions. In his own way, he was prepared to stimulate a Mormon renaissance.

Tragedy struck the young and otherwise happy couple when Merle got pregnant and gave birth to their first child, Laurel Colton Bennion, in November 1932 in Strasbourg. As Lowell was busy preparing for the defense of his dissertation—around the time when he first discovered the writings of Albert Schweitzer—their six-month-old baby girl swallowed an open safety pin. She was rushed to the hospital and the pin was removed, but she died of infection three days later. Although penicillin had been discovered in 1928, it wasn't available for civilian use until 1942. While both grieved deeply, Lowell described a peace that eventually came over him, while Merle remained disconsolate (Bradford 1995, 51–52). The death of their child was met with a combination of grief and fortitude and shaped their life with special compassion for inexplicable forms of suffering. This was not the only test he faced, but he already seemed to grasp that it was wiser and better to ask oneself what should be done rather than why things happen. Although Merle and Lowell carried a wound the rest of their lives, they returned to Utah to pursue the next phase undeterred from their path of high ideals.

After sending their deceased child home to Utah in a coffin, the couple astoundingly labored together on finishing Lowell's dissertation. Merle typed drafts and studied French with him, since that would be the language of his defense, while Lowell wrote, completed, and defended the 173-page dissertation by the end of 1933, just after Hitler had come to power in neighboring Germany. The young, intellectually gifted, and deeply faithful Bennion returned to the United States with the thought of maybe running for the US Senate or becoming a professor, but upon his return in 1934, he drew the attention of Apostle John Widstoe (Bennion 1985c, 8). Widstoe was Harvard-educated and well known for his LDS embrace of science, and he was an admirer of Bennion's father, Milton. Acting as the commissioner of education for the LDS Church, Widstoe extended an invitation to Lowell to serve as institute director, first at the University of Idaho in

Moscow. When Lowell hesitated, he offered instead that Lowell found a new institute at the University of Utah, which Lowell quickly accepted. This was the fourth LDS institute, and it warranted a private meeting with the current apostle, David O. McKay, the future president (1951–70) and a mentor who had married him and his wife, Merle. McKay offered simple wisdom for the job ahead, advice Bennion repeated throughout his life to his students. McKay said, "I don't care what you do or what you draw upon, but be true to yourself and loyal to the cause" (qtd. in Bradford 1995, 65). Widstoe met monthly with Lowell and his students during that next year, offering advice and entrusting Lowell with great confidence. Lowell faced times of contradiction and uncertainty and even storm-tossed waves of controversy, but, inspired by the examples of Widstoe and McKay, he met them with the confidence that the teachings of his church offered a set of ideals high and capacious enough to reconcile whatever conflicts might emerge.

After Lowell and Merle spent a two-year stint at the institute at the University of Arizona, T. Edgar Lyon joined Lowell as assistant director of the institute at the University of Utah in 1939. Shortly thereafter, Lowell published his first major work, *The Religion of the Latter-day Saints*, a textbook that, with additional revisions and expansions, served as a manual for college students for many years. As noted earlier, the book was published on the heels of a major address by J. Reuben Clark, then a member of the First Presidency, *The Charted Course of Church Education*, in 1938. Clark not only denounced ethics as a focus of religious education but also offered a stark contrast between secular, or what he calls "natural" ways of knowing, and the "spiritual" means by which the Holy Ghost testifies of eternal truth, independent of education and reason. In Clark's view, teachers like Beeley and now Bennion who were educated elsewhere risked becoming an elite class who were bringing back their very up-to-date training and "dos[ing] it upon us without any thought as to whether we needed it or not" (Clark 1938, 8). Clark himself was a complex blend of high educational aspiration and achievement and staunch anti-intellectualism.

This seeming contradiction was not new to Mormonism. Thomas Simpson aptly describes Brigham Young's fascinating "blend of intellectual prudishness and promiscuity" in the nineteenth century (Simpson 2016, 27). Even today in the LDS Church's institutions of higher education, secularism is deemed on one hand an accepted norm, even a desired source of inspiration and revelation, and, on the other, an alarming invasion against which the institutions must be safeguarded. The outside world was at once immense and alluring, maybe even necessary for Mormon purposes, but also small and insignificant by comparison, potentially deceptive or even antagonistic. Although Bennion offered a more moderate and balanced approach to secularism than what Clark had offered, Clark's speech today remains institutionally more influential than Bennion's manuals. This is despite the fact that he offered a more comprehensive and doctrinally principled approach to his belief in the value of intellectual curiosity than Clark's brief gloss of LDS doctrine and marked denunciation of intellectualism. It is not an overstatement to believe, as Terryl Givens asserts, that Clark's speech did more to "constrain the LDS Church's intellectual culture for coming generations" than any other speech of the century (Givens 2021, 50). It certainly helped to shape the currents that have contributed to Bennion's virtual anonymity today.[1]

To keep students engaged with the LDS Church and its doctrines, Bennion was intent on presenting them with an expansive rather than restrictive faith. He worried, contra Clark, that if spiritual knowledge was oversponsored or its distinctions from secular knowledge were overstated, believers would paint themselves into theological corners that could contradict empirical reality and lived experience. Because revelation in LDS theology is continuous, he chose to emphasize the unending and dialogic nature of revelation: "revelation is a response to man's thinking in man's language. . . . It's not all divine dictation" (Bennion 1985b, 105). If revelation is nothing but pure transmission of divine knowledge without translation and without struggle or imagination on the part of the believer, he didn't feel it could speak to the conditions of life sufficiently to inspire the moral growth for which it is intended. Bennion worried that without due acknowledgment of secular influence within religion itself, believers cannot find adequate explanation for differences of opinion among church leaders or even among fellow believers, except as betrayal. In other words, as we have since learned from Charles Taylor's insightful critique of secularism, overpolicing the boundaries between the sacred and secular may fail to acknowledge their mutual influence and interdependence (2007).

In one sense, he was guilty as charged: Bennion returned from Europe believing that his education could assist Mormonism in finding ways to gain traction in the world, to be useful to it and to benefit from it, but he also firmly hoped that this could be accomplished without being *of the world*, by remaining faithful to fundamental Christian principles. As more educators like Bennion obtained their advanced degrees outside Utah, higher education served, in the words of Matthew Bowman, "to translate the things America demanded of them into the language and imperatives of their own faith" (Bowman 2012, 153) and to heal what Thomas Simpson calls "the wounds of exile" (Simpson 2016, 2). Education elsewhere, of course, offered not only a chance to improve themselves but risked eroding the unique conditions of this peculiar religious community. Indeed, such was Clark's chief worry. Even as an independent observer, Thomas O'Dea concurred twenty years later that Mormonism's unique character needed intellectual openness but could potentially be undermined by it, and that its future viability depended on its ability to strike the right balance. When Bennion read O'Dea's study of 1957, he could see he was living in the midst of what O'Dea insightfully described as a "present state of prolonged but regularized crisis" (O'Dea 1957, 240).

This ambivalence within the Church of Jesus Christ of Latter-day Saints was not entirely unique. Throughout the nineteenth century and into the early decades of the twentieth, the biological and earth sciences, philosophy, psychology, sociology, and history and the emergence of higher criticism had all presented challenges to traditional understandings of the moral authority of the Bible and of Christianity in the world. One response, developed by Christian modernists practicing a progressive "new theology," was to assume some validity to the claims of these various disciplines and to develop theological responses to meet the challenges they presented. Walter Rauschenbusch's monumental *Christianity and the Social Crisis* of 1907, for example, helped lay the groundwork for a modernist, liberal Christianity, committed to the "social gospel," a commitment to an education and life of ethical concern for the here and now. Quite a different impulse was to protect Christianity against secular infiltrations. The twelve volumes of *The Fundamentals* published by multiple authors between 1910 and 1915 denounced liberal Christianity (including, interestingly, Mormonism) and the ethical orientation of liberal Christianity and laid the foundation for contemporary conservative Christian fundamentalism and its emphasis on preserving the unique doctrinal claims of Christianity. This emerging division eventually led to the secularization of most of the country's originally religious institutions of higher education, on one hand, and, on the other, to the increasingly disenfranchised and rare religious institutions, including the various campuses of Brigham Young University today, that would hold their ground and, in some cases, dig deeper trenches of resistance (Rauschenbusch 2008; Torrey 1972).

At stake for many theologians in these debates was the position of God vis-à-vis the world. If God was immanent in the world and its cultures, as Christian modernists saw it, then the humanities and the sciences were not the road to secular perdition but indispensable for a higher knowledge of the truth and for building God's kingdom on the earth. Bennion was part of a wave of LDS academics who shared this sensibility, including his immediate boss, Frank West, who oversaw church education from 1936 to 1953; his compatriots at the University of Utah T. Edgar Lyon, Daryl Chase, Sterling McMurrin, and George Boyd; and several faculty members at Brigham Young University, including Russel Swensen and Sydney Sperry. These were the lay inheritors of an expansive LDS vision of the spiritual value of secular education that had been articulated in the early twentieth century by such church leaders as B. H. Roberts and James Talmage, and later John Widstoe, during what Matthew Bowman has aptly called "the golden age of Mormon theology" (Bowman 2012, 163).

If, however, God was not immanent but transcendent over and above the historical unfolding of cultures and human understanding, secular learning was at best necessary for utilitarian ends, but also was potentially dangerous, if not already deserving of outright condemnation. Ernest Wilkinson, who served as the president of Brigham Young University and of the entire Church Educational System from 1951 to 1971, had a preference for this more conservative position, as did Clark, as we saw. Other similarly conservative positions were assumed by leaders such as Joseph Fielding Smith and Ezra Taft Benson (Quinn 2002; Harris 2020).

A religion replete with supernatural claims but possessed of a radically open theology, Mormonism didn't track perfectly with national trends even if it was often interpreted by its own practitioners through such a lens (Bowman 2012, 181). It proved inhospitable to the more extreme liberal elements, but it still struggled for harmony between its own complex blend of fundamentalism and modernism, a harmony that Bennion spent his career seeking to articulate. While LDS teachings about the afterlife moved and inspired the believing educator, Bennion insisted that they were designed to help believers attend to the specific and concrete circumstances

of contemporary life. The irony of various expressions of anti-intellectualism in the LDS Church was that they narrowed the religious life to the
not-always-reliable assurances available in the conceptual realm of human
experience. For Bennion, religion was life and, thus, he saw divinity as
both immanent *and* transcendent and religion as a call to a higher plane
of existence but one that begins with ethical commitments and meaningful
experiences here and now.

Experiences of service, then, were indispensable to a religious education
and to lifelong worship, especially in an increasingly secular world that
might appear to be antagonistic to religious life. Service helped to diminish the sense of differences over which secularists and religionists alike
tended to agonize, differences that too easily became false dichotomies.
He sought to diminish polarization by avoiding labels and the rhetoric of
culture wars and instead consistently dressed his thought in the principles
and values of Christian living derived directly from scripture. This allowed
him to engage the issues of his day without appearing to pit his students
either against the church or against the reality of the issues themselves.

Endowed with the gifts of an effective and passionate communicator,
Bennion thrived in the environment of the college campus and relished
the role his courses and the institute played for the thousands of students
that came under his influence in those years. When the institute began, he
stated four purposes for it in a brochure he published: to assist in answer-
ing student questions about their own religious thinking and philosophy
of life; to acquaint students with the role of religion and religious leaders
in the formation of their civilization; to increase students' knowledge of
the place of Mormonism in a global context and to strengthen their faith
in the Restored Gospel; and to offer a social center for Latter-day Saint
students (Bradford 1995, 64–65). Ample evidence shows that the many
students who came under his and Lyon's influence over the next twenty-
seven years felt that the institute accomplished these purposes astonish-
ingly well. One student summarized his experience in this way: "Going
to the Institute was more than just getting my religious beliefs reinforced.
It was an expansive and adventuresome experience" (Bradford 1995, 115).
Taught to creatively seek opportunity to live meaningfully on behalf of
others, students found the institute to be a kind of moral and intellectual
laboratory to integrate education and faith and to practice their religion
more fully.

Rather than being quick to blame wayward students when they seemed to lack faith, Bennion assumed the responsibility to improve what he offered. His was a student-centered approach that assumed that "students no longer involved in church activity have not enjoyed the true religious experience. Religion has just not been integrated into life and thought" (Bradford 1995, 63). His willingness to meet students where they were and his authenticity attracted students to his classes and to his office for counsel and advice. They followed him too into the community, where, instead of keeping himself at the center of their attention, he taught them to make the least advantaged more central to their own pursuit of meaning. The scriptures remained front and center as he empowered students to develop their own thinking and interpretations in a principled way and to make the gospel relevant to the conditions of their lives. Although a sober man of quiet disposition who preferred to let others speak first, he possessed a quick and dry wit and had an unmistakable sparkle in his eye. His love for others was expressed more by deed than by word, and it wasn't overly sentimental or physically affectionate. While this demeanor sometimes frustrated others who needed more overt signs of approval, his love was decidedly focused on principle and service rather than on mere feeling.

His parenting style as well was long on example but perhaps short on intimacy. During the institute years, Lowell and Merle had four sons, Ben, Doug, Steve, and Howard and then a daughter, Ellen. His daughter noted that even though he was often gone serving others, she and her brothers came to appreciate and emulate the values that guided his life because they at least knew that he lived what he taught and that "he was true to himself" (Goldberg, Newell, and Newell 2018, 212). That is, although his rising reputation and commitment to service often limited time at home and left his children occasionally wanting a more intimate and personal relationship with their father, it was clear that they were loved and that they loved in return. Four of the five children became educators and Howard, a nurse. Son Steve served as president of Ricks College, Snow College, and Southern Utah University.

As a gay man, Howard struggled to follow the pattern of his siblings and ultimately decided not to serve a mission. When he finally shared his sexuality with his parents in the late 1960s, Lowell and Merle were devastated. Of course, homosexuality was not well understood or accepted in the broader US society at the time, let alone in a devout LDS community and family. Nevertheless, Lowell and Merle remained loving and fully committed to Howard's well-being, especially after a suicide attempt and some false starts in his educational endeavors. After developing a profession in nursing and working for a time in Hawaii, he returned to Utah, and, as an indication of the strength of their mutual affection, he and his partner built a home on his parents' property. When local church leaders took action to excommunicate Howard, Lowell insisted on being a witness, pleading with the lay leaders to show compassion and mercy. Although Lowell's plea went unheeded, his father's defense would profoundly affect Howard for the rest of his life. Lowell eventually became public about his distaste for the practice of excommunication.

In 1949, at the invitation of Sterling McMurrin, a graduate student in sociology, Bennion, T. Edgar Lyon, Obert C. Tanner, and other male LDS academics and intellectuals began holding regular meetings to explore various dimensions of LDS theology, a group known as the "Mormon Seminar" but also more affectionately known as "The Swearing Elders." It is not clear if the gender exclusion was by design or by default, but it did exclude students and the male dominance stuck. Like larger forums that would proliferate in the coming decades—such as *Dialogue*, *Sunstone*, the Mormon History Association, and the many online forums today—this group sought to meet the needs of a growing number of LDS academics who wanted to make sense of their faith tradition in light of their education. The group met for the next six years and explored a wide range of topics by inviting scholars from inside and outside the LDS Church to speak about their areas of expertise, especially as they might relate to LDS belief and culture. It was in embryo what would become known in the 1990s as Mormon Studies, characterized by a generous spirit of inclusion, a concern for social morality, and a desire to explore the fruits of a scholarly inquiry into the LDS experience. The group raised concern among more conservative members of the church hierarchy, some of whom wanted to see it disbanded, but David O. McKay offered protection. McMurrin and Tanner were both close friends of Bennion and had similarly pursued the academic life with high ideals, and the three shared a deep admiration for each other, even though they each took different paths over time in relation to the LDS Church.[2] All three believed in the value of independent, intellectually rigorous, and loving criticism from within the institution and experienced similar institutional resistance to their efforts, even though

Bennion remained the most orthodox of the three. Bennion cherished the stimulation of their conversations to the end of his life, despite or maybe because of the differences.

The crosswinds that existed at the time of Lowell's first hire at the institute continued to blow when, in 1951, David O. McKay became the first president of the Church of Jesus Christ of Latter-day Saints with a college degree, the same year the conservative Ernest Wilkinson became president of Brigham Young University. Only two years later, in an effort to unify all church schools, Wilkinson assumed additional responsibility for the Church Education System (CES) with director authority over all institutes as well. These developments created both opportunities and challenges for Bennion. In 1958, McKay invited Bennion to speak about marriage to the priesthood session of General Conference, a rare exception to the normal practice of choosing speakers from among the full-time leadership, and McKay continued to offer direct and personal support and counsel to Bennion. Bennion was later invited again to speak in General Conference in 1968 about education.

In 1954, however, at a convention of instructors in CES, Bennion found himself at odds with two members of the Quorum of the Twelve Apostles, Elder Mark E. Peterson and Elder Joseph Fielding Smith. Peterson elaborated on a rationale for banning the priesthood to all men of African descent that was based on the presumption of a sin committed by black people in the premortal existence. As early as 1849 to fellow church leaders and later in 1852 before the Utah territorial legislature, Brigham Young departed from Joseph Smith's view that the potential of African Americans was determined more by environment than by inherited essence and offered a belief in the black race as cursed, which justified racial hierarchies and the ban from the priesthood that he eventually instituted for all men of African descent in the LDS Church (Reeve 2017, 146). By the time David O. McKay assumed the presidency, it was clear that he and others did not feel authorized to overturn the ban without a revelation. The explanation of a premortal judgment had gained popularity among some leaders and members, even though it was unscriptural. In Bennion's judgment, the theory of premortal judgment was morally repugnant because it took a policy that had unclear origins in revelation and that went against the grain of accepted doctrines about the equality and dignity of all God's children and added insult to injury by blaming the victims of white supremacist attitudes *for* those attitudes. The ban may have needed a revelation to be overturned, but for Bennion, as long as justifications continued to sound quasi-revelatory and until and unless prejudice abated in the church, the revelation would never come.[3]

Lowell rose to speak and shared the story of a student who had asked him a question that he now posed to Elder Peterson: "If Negroes sinned, what sin could they commit for which a merciful God—as you speak of, Brother Peterson—would not be willing to forgive, if they repented?" (Bradford 1995, 132). He may have felt emboldened to ask this question because he had similarly asked President McKay in the private meeting described earlier in this chapter what justice there was in a punishment for a sin of which someone could never be cognizant. His lifelong impression from his conversation with McKay was that the prophet was sympathetic and that strong difference of opinion among the church hierarchy was the chief obstacle to overturning the ban. Although Peterson dug in on his position, Bennion's questions had exposed the weakness of the ban's justifications.

Later at the same CES gathering, Joseph Fielding Smith spoke about science and insisted that the earth was only six thousand years old, and again Bennion spoke. He asked if he could explain his own method of teaching on such questions to see whether Smith would agree it was sound. He said that instead of pitting science against religion, he had opted to speak fervently and openly of his own spiritual convictions about God, Jesus Christ, and Joseph Smith's role in the Restoration. He added that when science engages in overreach and tries to deny the existence of God, he will defend religion, "but when it comes down to details like the exact process of how God created Adam on this earth and brought forth things on the earth, I say in the name of religion we don't know, and also that science has not come far enough along to be convinced either. . . . From either standpoint we don't have the final answer. However, I try not to get the student agitated against science, get him prejudiced against geology, and get him to feel that he has to choose between some science and the gospel of Jesus Christ" (Bradford 1995, 133). Bennion referred to his own son, whose interest in geology should not pit him against the gospel (Bennion 1985b, 95). Smith remained firm in his stance.[4] Bennion's questions led to further discussion at the CES meeting about when church leaders were speaking authoritatively and when they were expressing opinion, a discussion that did not result in a clear answer.

As is evident from the record of that incident, Lowell's style was not confrontational, but he was also not easily intimidated by authority. Perhaps because he knew and was loved by a handful of church leaders, including the president, and because his own father had often hosted leaders at dinner in his home, he was not one to idolize or cower in the face of authority or one to demonize or dehumanize a leader over a difference of opinion. In these interactions with Peterson and Smith, he kept the focus on a problem he invited them to help him solve rather than on any apparent errors he or others might have believed they were making. Sociology and his own experience had taught him that institutions too easily lose sight of the ways in which ideas and practices affect real human lives, but he also understood that becoming a gadfly would only distract both him and the institution from fundamental responsibilities. Toward the end of his life, he wrote, "I have perhaps a rather unorthodox view of the humble as those who feel no need to continually take their personal pulse, analyze how they feel about a given topic, or develop and express an opinion on every item of conversation" (Bennion 1990, 26–27).

Bennion learned from his study of Weber that institutions too easily rigidify in the face of opposition and produce quasi-official, albeit erroneous, dogma and thereby do even worse damage to individuals. He explained, "I've never been a bandstand arguer for the blacks[,] . . . but when I was called upon to express my views on the subject, when it was natural and appropriate, I expressed myself freely and honestly. I didn't feel like carrying on a campaign to embarrass anybody or the Church. *I thought that would eliminate any chance to be influential*" (Bennion 1985c, 10, emphasis added). Throughout his manuals and other books, Bennion sought to clarify the terms of integrity to which both individuals and institutions should aspire. He clearly believed that justifications for the priesthood ban that eschewed white responsibility and claims about the age of the earth that denied science would ultimately not meet the standard of such integrity. Identifying hypocrisy, however, was not an end in itself. Integrity required not only healthy criticism but even heavier doses of continual work to serve those aggrieved and to shed the outlying behavior or belief. If Weber was a man who understood such bureaucratic dynamics and tensions exceptionally well in theory, Bennion was a man of exceptional character who confronted and navigated around them in direct practice.

Bennion continued to teach as he had, seeking a holistic and healthy balance of intellectual and spiritual growth in his students. He produced in 1955 one of his most popular manuals, this time a Sunday school text, *Introduction to the Gospel*, that remained in use until the late 1960s. It was an astute and gracefully written approach to the spiritual and doctrinal foundations of Latter-day Saint religious practice and belief. In 1959, he published perhaps his greatest work, *Religion and the Pursuit of Truth*, for institute classes. The book summarized what he had been teaching for years and offered a clear-eyed understanding of the role religion could play in the holistic formation of the college student. It remains a remarkable testament to his high confidence in the rationality and moral power of the Latter-day Saint faith.

Bennion's exceptional contributions to his church notwithstanding, he was not safe from attack. Ernest Wilkinson was a deeply conservative man who was not above spying on his own faculty for communist or atheistic tendencies and wanted to purge CES of any influences he deemed danger- ous. Wilkinson was gathering a list of potentially problematic instructors who wouldn't toe the doctrinal line, and Bennion was on it. He earned a place on the list presumably because he voiced concerns about the priest- hood ban, defended science, and took a nuanced and public stance on the contingency of revelation. Bennion was also unwilling to proselytize the institute or pursue college credit for institute classes, two goals of special concern to Wilkinson. Bennion preferred to protect the freedom of volunteer association and to avoid unnecessary religious conflicts at the university. In the end, it is hard to understand all that motivated Wilkin- son. He knew Bennion to be a man of great faith and integrity and seemed genuinely to admire him, but he was perhaps jealous of or perplexed by his quiet and principled approach to the moral life and the popularity he enjoyed among his students. He eventually offered Bennion a position at Brigham Young University, most likely as a strategy to diminish Bennion's autonomy and direct influence on students, and Bennion refused. In any case, before the Board of Trustees, Wilkinson successfully used Bennion's failure to take attendance or issue grades as justifications for removing him.

By 1962, Bennion was out as institute director. The University of Utah quickly offered the immensely popular teacher a position as assistant dean of students and as director of a government-sponsored program to assist juvenile delinquents, positions he seems to have gladly accepted. He also eventually began teaching sociology part-time, an opportunity that led to his promotion to full professor. Bennion strongly disagreed with his ouster from the institute, of course, and was unhappy that Wilkinson never offered an adequate explanation for it, and Bennion was somewhat baffled by McKay's apparent neutrality. He told his son Steve at the time, however, "I am glad to be home again to get things done. I am a poor spectator of life. My satisfactions lie in *creation, service*, and trying to keep my *integrity*" (Bradford 1995, 183; emphasis in original). As the news spread, however, letters of protest and alarm came pouring into church headquarters, and Bennion's life story to this day is more often known for this event than for any other, a fact that bothered him and his children, especially after the publication of his official biography by Mary Bradford in 1995 brought the details to light. Perhaps it tells us something of the private nature of the disappointment he experienced, however, that, sometime shortly after his dismissal, he recorded an experience of seeing Jesus Christ at the foot of his bed, which brought him great peace (Bradford 1995, 175). Even though he lamented the loss of connection with students in the way the institute had facilitated for more than twenty-eight years, he was able to embrace the opportunities for service ahead of him.

Just two summers prior to his dismissal, and with the help of loyal friends who acted as donors, Lowell launched the boys' ranch that would occupy his summers for the next twenty-five years. The ranch was inspired by his own experience as a young man in the summers of 1923 and 1924, when he went to work at the Utah-Nevada border with his uncle and lived in primitive conditions and did hard physical labor outdoors. He called it the "best summer" of his life "in terms of influence on my values and life" (Bradford 1995, 20). Convinced by his experience working with delinquents that hard work and service could straighten out even the most crooked and, concerned that American youth were increasingly distracted by frivolities, he wanted a place where he could inspire the development of the whole person inside and out, away from the distractions of an American adolescence.

The not-for-profit ranch, exclusively for boys ages twelve to fifteen years old, was in Victor, Idaho. and was guided more by moral principle than by religious doctrine or by rewards, ceremony, and achievement. The boys were taught the principles and values associated with hard work, service, and a commitment to excellence and they were then simply expected to work hard for four hours every morning after a rigorously judged morning cleanup, without complaint. At the end of a four-week term, a generous $50 check (about $400 in today's economy) would arrive at home. The work included service in the community of Teton Valley, building and maintaining the facilities of the ranch, weeding in the garden, and kitchen and laundry duty. Afternoons were spent in recreation and evenings in discussion and debate about social and political topics. Although he insisted the ranch wasn't for troubled youth, he would admit and work with anyone if there was space. Misbehaving boys were often sent to weed with Bennion in the garden, where he would teach the art of gardening with Zen-like patience and form special bonds of trust. Often without direct instruction about the misbehavior, it diminished.

The ranch was a harbinger of his growing preference for praxis rather than theory. Ten years after leaving the institute, he left the academy definitively. He began service in 1972 as director of the Community Services Council (CSC) in downtown Salt Lake City and ran unsuccessfully for the state legislature that same year. He led the CSC until 1988. The CSC was a private nonprofit, initially sponsored by Community Chest and later by United Way, that functioned as a catalyst and facilitator for more than 140 government and private agencies that served citizens with health and social needs. The council did more facilitating and administrating than Bennion wanted because, despite its efforts, many citizens lacked vital services. His leadership transformed the council by meeting those needs directly and expanding services previously offered by its many partners. One beneficiary was what became known as the food bank, which had existed under the name of Salt Lake Charity since the early 1900s but was transformed and expanded throughout the state under Bennion's leadership and eventually into the intermountain region (Utah Food Bank). Some have argued that Bennion's insistence on service to the community helped to broaden the LDS welfare program's focus on self-reliance to include the notion of community and humanitarian service, which is now more the norm. As Bennion pithily summarized those years, "I used to teach religion; now I practice it" (Bradford 1995, 265).

The last decades of Bennion's life saw a steady stream of what he called his "little books" written for a general LDS readership and published by Deseret Book and a number of small independent publishers. He also published articles in two independent journals, *Dialogue* and *Sunstone*, that were thriving during those decades. Prior to the age of the internet, podcasts, and blogging, it wasn't always clear where an independent mind like Bennion's, no longer directly conscripted by his church and no longer affiliated with the academy, could find venues for publication and outlets for influence. He never ventured into the publication of formal academic works, even though he occasionally expressed regret for not having done so.

Reading these books today, one gets the impression of a mind continually possessed of a singular and important vision of the universality of Mormonism but also possessed of the conviction that such universality was perpetually at risk. Presumably, he felt the need to provide such supplementary books because the Sunday curriculum and the broader educational system were neither providing sufficient integration of faith and intellect that he long championed nor the social morality he felt members needed. It wasn't exactly the case that the church opposed efforts like Bennion's. In many ways, his efforts were welcomed. In its increasing size and bureaucracy and international reach as an institution, it had become more and more difficult to provide the kind of carefully tailored and nuanced guidance members needed. This left those who most desired to serve the church with their intellectual skills in a kind of no-man's land of uncertainty about their place in the institution, as happened to Bennion, since their offerings can be adopted or dropped at will. Free to write and publish more independently, Bennion nevertheless never published a word that was anything but faithful to the fundamental tenets of his religion, despite the cloud of suspicion that the LDS Church had created around his efforts when it inexplicably blacklisted him from ever publishing formally for the church after the 1960s (Bradford 1995, 334).

Bennion passed away on February 21, 1996, after a long fight with Parkinson's that had sapped his physical strength but not his vigorous mind. Gordon Hinckley, then president of the church, spoke at his funeral. Hinckley and Bennion had been neighbors for many years, and in many ways, Hinckley's thoughtful, frank, and humane style as a leader shared the tone and wisdom of Bennion and was the fruition of that generation of church figures who were shaped by those early and hopeful days of a brief Mormon renaissance. It wasn't, however, to Bennion's thought that Hinckley pointed but to his modesty and commitment to service. Hinckley noted that he had observed the cars in the parking lot for the funeral and thought to himself, "Lowell Bennion never drove a car as good as the poorest of these." To Lowell, Hinckley said, "a car was just a means to get somewhere to do good" (qtd in Bennion 1996, 171).

Bennion's Legacy Today

It is a cliché to think of great minds as ahead of their time, but in many ways it was true of Bennion. In the early 1970s, before the Church of Jesus Christ of Latter-day Saints reversed the ban on men of African descent in the priesthood and fully two decades before it took steps institutionally to condemn racism, he argued unambiguously that "Latter-day Saints should be in the forefront of the battle for equal civil rights for all groups in society" (England 1988, 252). He taught and practiced the value of humanitarian service, decades before the church ramped up its humanitarian efforts and before humanitarian missions became common and full-time proselyting missionaries began dedicating a portion of their time to humanitarian service. Decades before crises over climate change and vaccines that would emerge in Christian communities across the country, he was an early and consistent defender of scientific literacy as necessary "to realize the values and purposes postulated by our religious faith" (Bennion 1959, 115). Before the internet, the smartphone, and ubiquitous streaming services, he argued that "we are too busily engaged in being entertained" (Bennion 1996, 111) and that "we are unchristian and inhumane to live in luxury in a world where so many lack adequate food, clothing, and shelter, let alone medical attention and education" (Bennion 1988, 44). He named institutionalism, authoritarianism, self-righteousness, and dogmatism as the "illegitimate children of religion" in 1959, only to witness over the course of his life his community's struggle with these temptations that continue to afflict the culture (1959, 116–18).

History has borne out the fact that he was almost invariably on the right side of things, but Bennion's goal was never to be right but to do good, to make a real difference. When the ban on the priesthood of men of African descent was finally lifted in 1978 after more than three decades of effort and communication with church leaders, he was asked whether he felt exonerated. His answer was simply "No, I have lots else to think about" (Goldberg et al. 2018, 199). His daughter Ellen insisted that this was the secret to his ability to move on after he was let go as director of the institute in 1962 (Goldberg et al. 2018, 211) and, I would argue, the secret to his longevity and persistence in the face of slow and sometimes nonexistent change.

Nevertheless, it would be inaccurate to think of him as a forward thinker. He was decidedly old-fashioned. A writer loath to overcomplicate things and committed to the moral purpose of thought, he never dressed his writings in anything but the language and rhetoric of scripture, especially the Sermon on the Mount and the ethical teachings of the Old Testament prophets, which is perhaps one reason that he is seen by some as perhaps too pedestrian. The deeper and more disturbing question that we might ask, however, is why the Christian fundamentals Bennion championed ever grew out of fashion or became intellectually uninspiring. When asked what he would choose as an epitaph for his own tombstone, he quoted his favorite scripture from Micah 6:8: "What doth the Lord require of thee, but to do justly, and to love mercy, and to walk humbly with thy God" (KJV; Goldberg et al. 2018, 167). It certainly never occurred to Bennion that such a scripture was deserving of anything but a lifetime of high thinking.

As an educator who read widely, Bennion's thought was not entirely *sui generis*. Tracing his bibliographical sources is difficult because of his commitment to writing accessible books with minimal footnotes and citations, but it cannot be mere coincidence that his philosophies resonate so well with more the moderate wing of progressive theology in American Christianity that was increasingly ethical in its orientation and that downplayed the primacy of belief and of salvation. For more moderate theologians, the emphasis came not from a desire for secularization motivated by shame about Christianity's ontological claims but from a desire to shore up the viability of religion in the modern world. We know he was a devotee of Max Weber and Albert Schweitzer—and Rauschenbusch, Charles Briggs, Theodore Munger, Henry Churchill King, Hermann Lotze, Albrecht Ritschl, and George Coe all seem likely influences, if not thinkers who at least prepared the ground he would sow. His thought is remarkably consistent with the values that have guided the Jesuit order and Jesuit institutions of higher learning and with the theologies that have inspired various campaigns for social reform, including abolition and civil rights and environmental conservation (Jesuits 2022). One cannot escape the suspicion, however, that Bennion was a truly original Latter-day Saint thinker, one nurtured by the very exceptionalist tendencies of Latter-day Saint education that he both perpetuated and sought to mitigate. A descendant of polygamist Latter-day Saint pioneers and the child of an educator whose own strong ethical approach to religious education and deeply religious and humble character was a paramount influence on his son, Bennion was a child of an organic Mormonism that always sought fidelity to its peculiar origins even as it sought to broaden its reach.

Besides, there was significant overlap between Protestant modernism and Mormonism in their shared disavowal of original sin and optimism about human destiny, the perceived partnership between human agency and divine providence, the blurring of the sacred and the secular and the opening of multiple channels of revelation, and a desire for new political and social order (Simpson 2016, 100).[5] Christian modernism offered an understanding, very familiar to Latter-day Saints, of the need for continuing revelation in light of present circumstances. William Hutchison summarizes this theology, well expressed by the late-nineteenth-century theologian Charles Briggs, thus: "God had refrained from presenting in the Bible a complete system of theology, and had instead arranged that the church in each era should have only so much of the truth as it needs. Correspondingly, God had decided, for the purpose of revelation, to make use of the various languages of humanity instead of creating a 'holy language'" (Hutchison 1992, 92). As we will see, Bennion draws almost identical conclusions from his reading of not only the Bible but also the *Doctrine and Covenants* and the *Book of Mormon*. Indeed, what is striking about Bennion is that even as this era of Christian modernism faded and had little impact on contemporary Mormonism, he remained dedicated to its insights without breaking from Latter-day Saint orthodoxy as did others, including his peers Sterling McMurrin and O. C. Tanner.

In the end, Christian modernism could take a thoughtful and believing Latter-day Saint only so far. While Christian modernism grew increasingly suspicious of miracles and of the supernatural, Smith's modernistic revelations remained inseparable from the story of their not-so-modern supernatural origins. Smith restored a Christianity that revealed a God in the flesh even as it insisted on the contingent nature of human understanding of the divine and the need for continual revelation. Mormonism, in other words, would sooner or later need to establish its own equipoise between its modern and antimodern impulses, even as the ground of American modernity beneath continued to shift. Mormonism's progressive theology continues to be well suited for the modern world even as its supernatural boldness stands out as an unwelcome or disrespected fact, like some embarrassing skeleton in the Mormon family closet. This contradiction has tended to trouble Latter-day Saint discourse, and Bennion was a front-row witness to and even a victim of the crosswinds at the highest levels of church leadership that it caused, but it was both the challenge and opportunity that Bennion embraced.

Bennion was a genuinely Latter-day Saint educator, faithful to Mormonism's own doctrinal heritage but eager to build bridges to redress the world's problems and thereby simultaneously curate, revitalize, and expand the unique claims of Mormonism as an increasingly global phenomenon. What Bennion offered during his lifetime and still offers today is a uniquely Latter-day Saint answer to the problems of modernity—particularly the role of belief in the realms of the sacred and the secular, the relationship between belief and ethical practice, and the role, therefore, of religious education today—that have polarized American Christianity and Mormonism itself since Mormonism's founding in 1830.

There is more political polarization today in America and in the Latter-day Saint community than in Bennion's lifetime, making it ever more challenging for Latter-day Saints to define the value of religious education. Latter-day Saint youth continue to value higher education and pour into colleges across the country. Although the various church-owned campuses remain among the most popular destinations, religious education there remains chiefly centered on the teaching of doctrine and has left largely unrealized the kind of integration that Bennion had advocated. Moreover, thousands more LDS youth who attend non-LDS public and private schools throughout the country rely on institutes that are often more helpful for social interaction than for intellectual and spiritual symbiosis. Latter-day Saint educators continue to debate the merits and dangers of secular education, of the natural and physical sciences, the usefulness of philosophy and theology, and the relevance of contemporary social and political life to gospel living. They are faced with the perennial question, Is religious education a Christian defense against or a Christian embrace of the world? Perhaps the debate is a perennial and inevitable one, but Latter-day Saint students, consequently, continue to hear and experience ambivalence about the spiritual necessity of secular learning. Consequently, integration is still hard to come by, and the crisis, as O'Dea correctly surmised, remains "regularized" (1957, 240).

In other words, many of the problems that worried him—the tendency for religion to become overly focused on feckless feeling at the expense of reason and an ethical orientation to the world outside the church, its tendency to promote perfectionism and a focus on salvation at the expense of a dedication to service and improvement here and now, and its failure to become a welcoming space for all classes and races of people—remain struggles in contemporary Latter-day Saint life. Mormonism has been affected by the great struggle of identity politics in the early twenty-first century, even as it has also sought to resist it. The kind of focus on service that Bennion championed seems to be one way through this particular challenge. Moreover, because young people today seem to find claims to truth less interesting than engagement in good causes, Bennion's legacy of a rational and ethical Mormonism deserves renewed attention.

Bennion sought to be a midwife to a Mormonism that he passionately believed could and should transcend the limitations implied by his religion's marginalization and marked peculiarity. The way forward for Bennion was always by allowing the pressures and contradictions of the present context to bring out the best in Mormonism. As he put it in his General Conference address of 1968, "It seems to me that we need to reflect deeply upon the gospel of Jesus Christ in terms of its great fundamentals, and then we need to relate those fundamentals to the issues of the day" (England 1988, 196). The issues he mentioned in that talk included "air pollution, water pollution, crime, delinquency, family disorganization, war, racial strife. The resolution of these problems calls for training, as well as for character and faith" (England 1988, 193). He was incorrigibly hopeful that Mormonism could respond to such challenges and would indeed shine, if only it weren't hampered by its own exceptionalist protectionism. Mormonism was right to want to be unique, but he warned that peculiarity should not come at the expense of a primary commitment to the highest principles of loving mercy and doing justly found in all religions.

Bennion preferred a kind of practical but speculative theology to apologetics precisely because it would be, in his view, more effective in balancing Mormonism's uniqueness with its desire for universal relevance. Apologetics to him was a defensive and exceptionalist posture that sought to protect ideas, whereas theology, at least the kind he tried to practice, could focus instead on moral relevance in a contemporary context. It was, after all, an act of faith to believe that religion didn't need to be divorced or protected from lived experience and contemporary life, or from reason. A rational faith requires a theology that explores the moral meaning of interpretation, lived experience, all the academic disciplines and education itself. It requires a theology that is self-critical enough to offer clear and unambiguous guidelines for avoiding its own excesses and dangers.

When faced with secular hostility, religion is tempted to fight back, but Bennion consistently warned that right belief, either religious or political, was not the correct emphasis of Christian morality; redressing, not merely diagnosing, the inadequacies of institutional life—whether inside or outside the church—was not only more consistent with Christian values but potentially more unifying. Bennion was a subtle and nuanced moralist. He was not afraid to decry error, but he knew that error had many causes, not all of them intentional, and that a part of one's moral approach should be a recognition that institutions and their policies are by virtue of the very nature of the human condition insufficient but also deserving of compassion and supplementary service. Christianity could not be the political antidote to the policy failures of the secular world if it could not find the courage to accept the moral weight of responsibility we collectively bear not just for injustices of a particular false idea or practice but for the injustices of life itself.

As Mormonism's greatest ethicist and its most successful and influential educator of the past century, Lowell Bennion offered a uniquely balanced philosophy of religious education that could still serve the Church of Jesus Christ of Latter-day Saints and American Christianity to mitigate the increasing polarization between secular and religious and liberal and conservative worldviews that distract believers from living up to the high call of service in Christian discipleship.

CHAPTER TWO

The Abundant Life

When Lowell Bennion first encountered the social sciences as a college student in the 1920s, he was introduced to a method for understanding and explaining the environmental and psychological factors that shape human behavior. It was, in other words, both an explanatory frame for understanding behavior and a method for changing it. It was also at times a deterministic line of inquiry that might conflict with a strictly moral view of human behavior that assumed the underlying condition of radical free choice. Resistance to the social sciences had previously been voiced in the late nineteenth century by such figures as the British polymath William Morris (1834–96), who reacted against a growing fanaticism around the emerging mechanistic and deterministic worldviews. Boston University theologian Borden Parker Browne (1847–1910) developed one brand of what became known as personalism in theology and philosophy and defended the idea of the human personality as the fundamental and irreducible category for evaluating all reality. Martin Buber (1878–1965) later articulated the dialogic nature of identity as communication between and among subjects in his famous *I and Thou* from 1923 (translated as Buber 1972), a model that helped resist the deterministic tendencies of the new social sciences.[1] New Thought, first appearing in the nineteenth century, continued to champion the divinity and power of individuals to shape their own destiny, a trend that culminated in various articulations of the prosperity gospel. One example was James Allen's 1902 book, *As a Man Thinketh*, that continued to enjoy currency among Latter-day Saint and other Christian readers throughout the twentieth century. Harry Emerson Fosdick's 1943 classic, *On Being a Real Person*, similarly championed the notion of the radical autonomy of the self. Such writers claimed the powers of self-reliance and what is now known as positive thinking or positive psychology as a refuge from and resistance to an increasingly bureaucratic, complex, and impersonal world.

Bennion's Mormonism attracted him to aspects of such philosophies, even as he also could see the value of a more scientific approach. He was persuaded that historical materialism was an insufficient thesis for understanding human history and human destiny, but, unlike many conservative Christian thinkers, he was unwilling to downplay the many ways in which material reality shapes and conditions human existence. What Bennion faced was bifurcation between theologically prizing the divine powers of self-direction and scientifically assessing the material and social conditions of human behavior. In the interest of a more integrated form of faith available to Latter-day Saints in the twentieth century, Bennion wanted a method for being devout and believing while also being detached and analytical. One reason for his interest in a middle ground was that, in his own cultural context, he had seen both the positive effects of energizing agency to assist individuals in overcoming obstacles and the negative tendency to use a philosophy of self-reliance to unfairly blame the victims of social, racial, and economic inequalities.

The work of Max Weber offered him a way of striking the right balance. Weber articulated a way to understand both the conditions that undeniably shape individual and collective behavior and the margin of freedom that individually and collectively we share to use agency and creativity to shape behavior more deliberately (Bennion 1933, 48). Weber insisted that how human beings articulated the meaning of their own experience—what Bennion called the individual's "'actual' subjective meaning"—could not be ignored nor should it be overrationalized for scientific or ideological reasons (Bennion 1933, 148). Influenced as they might be by material conditions, Weber seemed to suggest, human values and agency, even when based in supernatural views, had their own persuasive power over the direction of history.

This in turn argued against reductive or deterministic understandings of human history or human behavior, even if reason and science might yield insights into both. Bennion concurred with Weber that no purely objective interpretation of history was possible, in part because, as he wrote in his dissertation, "the objectivity of knowledge is limited by our ideas of value, which determine our interest in reality and our choice of ideal types. These ideas of value are subjective and irrational beyond scientific analysis." He added the paradoxical conclusion "If one acknowledges the subjective element and accounts for it, they can have a higher degree of objectivity in their research" (Bennion 1933, 43). The subjective and value-driven world of the private and intimate self defies scientific rationalization and reductionism and, from Bennion's Latter-day Saint perspective on the eternal nature of the human person, for good reason.

Matthew Bowman suggests that in the wake of polygamy's end, LDS thinkers, especially B. H. Roberts, John Widstoe, and James Talmage, had started to give special attention to the doctrine of the divine parentage of human beings in order to emphasize the concept of "eternal progression" and divine potential (Bowman 2012, 166). This doctrine helped Mormonism to gain traction in the modern world, as the LDS Church strove for greater assimilation after the end of polygamy, and especially with the era's Progressivism as it highlighted human perfectibility and expressed the confidence that "science, scholarship, and philosophy could help them better understand their religion" (Bowman 2012, 164). The premium Mormonism put on individual worth was fertile soil for Bennion to find his own method.

At the same time, however, Weber helped Bennion to avoid underestimating the ways in which external forces shape human behavior and personality. The more aware we become of such forces, he believed, the freer we might become, even if the freedom is never absolute. When Bennion first encountered Abraham Maslow's hierarchy of needs, published in 1943, he resonated deeply with the ethical orientation implied in Maslow's schema. Maslow argued that human psychology was grounded in a hierarchy of needs that begins at the physiological level, builds toward the experience of safety, love, and belonging, and reaches the apex of self-esteem and self-actualization, which were the most important purposes of human life. Maslow's schema implied for Bennion that working to improve the social and material conditions of others was just as important as taking full responsibility for one's own life. Both are necessary because both dignify the human person. (See Maslow 1954.)

Bennion's thought developed a fascinating blend of Latter-day Saint confidence in the importance and inviolability of human agency with astute and sobering insights into the significant ways in which, collectively, institutions and social structures can inhibit that agency. He was an unabashed defender of the human freedom and responsibility to define and live by chosen values—and hence of self-reliance and religious freedom—but he was concerned that religious values too easily become subservient to forces that undermine individuals' best intentions. In his own personal formulation, he "decided . . . to take full responsibility for what I think and feel and do, but to try to understand other people in terms of their background and environment and factors that enter into their lives" (Bennion 1985b, 45). He found a religious reason to be interested in sociology, in other words, since it could give him additional tools to unleash the "eternal progress" of human creativity and moral capacity in others. The key was to lead others to such waters through religious education.

The Quest of Selfhood

Bennion's own elaboration of Latter-day Saint doctrine about the eternal dignity of the individual, then, was always carefully balanced by a commitment to social morality. He did not see social morality, however, as a concept borrowed from secular philosophy but as central to Christian thought. Fetishizing personalism or individualism at the expense of the obligations we all have to collective life could be just as serious a form of secular overreach as fetishizing a scientific focus that lost sight of individual obligations and powers.

With that context in mind, perhaps we can best assess the significance of what he called "the enrichment of personality," which he insisted was God's "most creative endeavor in the universe" (Bennion 1940, 70). His goal was to unleash the passions in his students that could grant them a margin of freedom and power in the midst of the imposing circumstances of life. Such language was clearly indebted to personalism, but, more important, it resonated deeply with the religion's claims about the divine potential of human beings, a doctrine that he made a centerpiece of Latter-day Saint education. For Bennion, this enrichment begins with the individual choice of values that could shape and direct one's life toward higher ends. In 1978, he published a definitive summary of his belief in values in a book he considered his personal favorite, *The Things That Matter Most*. In it, he offers a hierarchy of values that resembled Maslow's hierarchy of needs. This difference between values and needs signaled

Bennion's particular emphasis on the creative and agentic dimensions of the individual life:

He does not insist that these should be everyone else's precise hierarchy of values because values are "personal and subjective" (Bennion 1978, 11). He argues, nevertheless, for the benefit of deliberately and creatively understanding and prioritizing one's values. The underlying argument is that a "significant and rewarding" life is one that intentionally creates an integrated balance of values (Bennion 1978, 11), rather than one merely determined or storm-tossed by circumstance. The freedom to choose what to value is the basis for the indispensable discovery of "a sense of individuality, a feeling of creativity, an assurance of measurable self-determination" (Bennion 1978, 20).

In *The Things That Matter Most*, he explains that human beings are essentially divided between the objective world of external reality and the subjective world of values, a distinction that had been operating in his thought since his dissertation on Weber. The objective world presses on us and imposes conditions and limitations, to the point where it is common for human beings to feel "powerless, expendable, contingent" (Bennion 1978, 20). "As a small entity in the vast universe," he explains, "I sense my contingency, my dependency on forces beyond my control. My life is hardly my own" (20). He insists, however, that human freedom starts not in material conditions but in the inner world of conscious thought, imagination, and desire. It is here, in this seat of the human personality, that we shape our inner life and create the possibility of shaping external reality in positive and fulfilling ways, thus establishing a deep and lasting sense of our value and purpose: "I make choices, I choose those things which I prefer, things I desire, things precious to me. I place value on them." In deciding what to value and how to live, "life becomes purposeful, hence meaningful" (20).

In chosen human values lies the margin of freedom in a vast universe of contingencies and material conditions where the human person finds and expresses herself. Despite the many forces of nature and society that act on Bennion, in living a life of chosen values, he says, "I feel alive. I affirm life with all my being" (Bennion 1978, 20). The work of cultivating an inner life, then, is deeply spiritual work and especially important in the context of a religious life since it is not uncommon that institutional norms end up supplanting this vital, inner work. To cultivate the inner life is nothing short of the opportunity to create the kingdom of God: "Truly, the kingdom of God is within us. It lies in our integrity, love, and other fine qualities of mind and heart. To cultivate the inner life is the way to self-fulfillment and the good life" (Bennion 1996, 9).

Again, however, Bennion did not mean to establish grounds for neglecting the material, institutional, and social conditions of life. In fact, it was a reminder of the principle on which collective life should be grounded. Institutions—churches, schools, and governments—would lose their integrity and do harm rather than their intended good if they failed to remain focused on the conditions that allow each human personality to flourish. In his 1983 book, *I Believe*, he summarizes his lifelong philosophy: "My first, central, and highest loyalty is to persons, both mortal and divine. Nothing else in religion, on earth or in the universe is quite as important. Nothing matters ultimately as much as what happens to persons and relationships between persons" (Bennion 1983, 63). His second loyalty, he further explains, "is to the principles of the gospel: to faith, repentance, justice, freedom, love and its many expressions—empathy, mercy, and forgiveness" (65). Finally, his third loyalty is to the Church of Jesus Christ of Latter-day Saints,

> not because it is unimportant, but because, in my judgment, it is instrumental to the other two loyalties already discussed. . . . The LDS church is not an end to be served, but an instrument through which together we may serve God and man. It is a fellowship, called and ordained of the Lord, blessed and empowered from on high, to inculcate the principles and spirit of the gospel into the lives of men. (Bennion 1983, 67)

If the enrichment of personality begins in this life, the abundant life that Christ promises his followers is, for Bennion, both a promise of a richer inner life and a deeper set of satisfactions in the present social world. The prospect of an abundant life isn't, in other words, merely a promise about salvation *from* life but in and through it. As he put it simply, "an abundant life is the fulfilled life, one that is fully engaged with mind and heart, reaching out to the world around us and to the people in it and living by faith in its divine origin and purpose" (Bennion 1990, 22). In the Book of Moses, Joseph Smith's inspired translation of Genesis, God declares that it is "my work and my glory to bring to pass the immortality and eternal life of man" (Moses 1:39). Bennion read this as not merely a declaration about the spiritual and postmortal destiny of human beings, as was the most common Latter-day Saint interpretation, but as a statement of God's vested interest in full self-realization for every person that begins here on earth. He often insisted that "the purpose of life will be found in life itself. That toward which man aspires is more life—*abundant and eternal life*" (Bennion 1940, 53).[2] We are all "here to develop their potentialities as children of God—that [we] might find joy" (Bennion 1959, 31). Happiness is the Latter-day Saint quest of selfhood that begins now:

> The beginning and end of life is to experience it deeply in all of its finest expressions. Self-realization or self-fulfillment—to be what nature and God intended us to be—appears to be the ultimate meaning of life. Salvation is a process of becoming, not a reward given us at the end of our journey or on judgment day. Life goes on and will continue. Let it be in search of meaning. Let it be for things that matter most. (Bennion 1978, 62)

Sin, then, was anything that compromises the abundant and integrated inner life: "The mind strives for unity; sin impairs that unity, weakening our sense of self" (Bennion 1985a, 73). Sin was often a symptom of a deeper problem that was for Bennion at least partially psychological and perhaps derived again from personalism, as he explained in *I Believe*: "Christ knew, as many students of human behavior have come to understand, that it is quite impossible for us to love our neighbor unless we have learned to love ourselves. And we cannot love ourselves if we are weak and divided" (Bennion 1983, 10). Sin is not only harmful action toward others but a form of self-division that violates our inner hunger for wholeness and puts us at risk of self-deception or self-hatred.

40

During the twentieth century, the social sciences often ventured into reductive or mechanistic explanations of behavior. Christian responses defended agency and the concept of sin but in so doing often ironically ended up mirroring such reductive thinking. To the degree that the social sciences implied that human behavior was rooted only in material or psychological conditions and was not agential, religious defenses often insisted that human misbehavior was always only a misuse of agency, which could easily become a self-condemning tautology: you sinned because, well, you chose the wrong thing. You are broken, in other words, because you don't work correctly. If the grounds for repentance were hard to identify in the social sciences, the ubiquity of the concept of repentance in Christian discourse only disguised its more fundamental mystery. Repentance, for Bennion, is not merely greater obedience or trying harder to be good but expanding and taking creative advantage of the freedom of the soul to attach itself to better things of value. As a believer works to cultivate new affections, old habits can begin to fade. Christian contemplative Thomas Keating developed a psychology of spirituality that resonated with Bennion's ideas in his 1992 classic, *Invitation to Love*: Repentance "means *to change the direction in which you are looking for happiness*" (1992, 9). Although this was not a commonly accepted definition of repentance in Mormonism, Bennion implies throughout his work that it could produce less shame and stimulate more willingness to love more bravely and creatively.

Nurturing the inner life and cultivating affection for good things, Bennion argued, would also increase a capacity to resist temptation. In *I Believe*, he wrote, "The way to find joy and freedom in gospel living is not to strive for the perfection of Deity here and now. Such a goal is immodest and impossible. Rather, let us become converted to the ideals the Savior taught; *let us fall in love with them and not be afraid to live by them* (Bennion 1983, 57, emphasis added). In other words, he was less interested in the self's purity and more interested in the self's integrity. "It is better to fight temptation indirectly," he explained, "to concentrate so thoroughly on the good things of life that there is not time or room for evil" (Bennion 1985a, 42). Emphasizing the love for high ideals instead of better compliance with commandments would shift away from shame and would "contribute richly to our sense of freedom" (Bennion 1983, 51). It is not surprising, then, that throughout his career he repeatedly decried the evils of perfectionism and offered this simple formula: "If you add up men's weaknesses and strengths, they come out even" (Bennion 1988a, 12). He concluded, "The tragedy of life is not to have sinned, but, having sinned, to accept defeat and henceforth to pine away our days in remorse. Matthew Cowley once said, 'Man is greater than all his sins.' Surely he is in the eyes of God; let him also be in his own eyes" (Bennion 1983, 33).

Bennion's concerns about perfectionism stemmed from his Weberian understanding that a concept like human perfectibility, so central to the Latter-day Saint idea of eternal progress and a common thread in early-twentieth-century Progressivism, could provide a powerful incentive to transform the material conditions of life, as historians have noted in the history of Latter-day Saint settlements in the American West, but could also, if not balanced with social morality, come at the expense of an inner sense of wholeness and satisfaction. An overvaluation of ends lends itself to a spirit of control and an increasing dependence on external conditions as measures of inner peace. His many conversations with young Latter-day Saints convinced him that perfectionism ironically doesn't inspire progress but a downward spiral of self-hatred that increasingly seeks rationalizations and superficial and external validations of the self. There was, as Bennion saw it, little purpose or joy in such self-defeating cycles. As he stated toward the end of his life, "Striving for perfection puts us on the horns of a dilemma. If we think we are succeeding, we run the risk of losing humility; if we know we are failing, we become discouraged. There is a better way" (Bennion 1996, 95). Or, as he once wryly put it, "One of the very real dangers in trying to be a good example is that we may think we are succeeding" (Bennion 1981, 60).

In his posthumous book, *How Can I Help?*, he gave special focus to this question that seemed to have grown more urgent in later years: "[the] New English Bible translation of Matt. 5:48 reads: 'Let there be no limit to your goodness even as the goodness of god knows no bounds.' . . . This view of perfection helps us to focus our attention on the possible instead of expending our energies in frustrating attempts to achieve the impossible" (Bennion 1996, 96–97). Bennion hoped that seeing perfection as a kind of integrity and wholeness would help to diminish the hunger to obtain things as compensation for our inadequacies and open the soul to the simple pleasures of life that should occupy the mind and motivate the affections. His better way was for students to drink deeply from simple and modest pleasures, a capacity he believed he learned in his years as a poor student in Europe (Bennion 1985b, 61): "Joy and abundant life come from living well in the present, focusing on each day's tasks and each day's satisfactions. Living largely in day-tight compartments can be more rewarding than being preoccupied with the past and/or future" (Bennion 1996, 102).

In his formula, gratitude quiets the noise of a compulsively active conscience that perpetually condemns the self. Gratitude and humility should pervade one's life feeling because they help one to see the giftedness of life:

> We make unconscious demands on life. We concentrate on our needs and unfulfilled desires and as a result often feel disappointed and frustrated. If we thought of life as a gift, we might not demand nearly as much from it. And if we lived more graciously, giving of ourselves more freely to the well-being of others, many of our personal concerns would disappear, and life would become easier for all. (Bennion 1996, 27)

The willingness to receive divine gifts of mercy and generosity facilitates this transition from a state of fallenness to a state of grace. Sin, then, is less a violation of a law and more a failure to receive the already offered gift of the abundant life, something that Latter-day Saint theologian Adam Miller has recently argued (Miller 2018a, 2018b).[3]

This isn't to say that Bennion ignored injustice. As noted earlier, the point of an autonomous and healthy spirituality and psychology is to increase one's joy and meaning in living in ethical concern for others. In one of the most potent summaries of his thought, in *The Religion of the Latter-day Saints*, he writes, "The religious life becomes the devotion of one's whole soul to the highest cause in the Universe—*co-operating with God in bringing to pass a more creative, joyful, eternal, God-like life for all men*" (Bennion 1940, 54, emphasis added).

Perhaps inspired by Maslow and by his intuitive sense of human psychology, he saw that such flourishing of human life required first meeting fundamental needs. In *Jesus the Master Teacher*, published during the later years of his life, he insisted that, "after food, water, and air" students need most of all,

1. Acceptance by others
2. Creative self-expression
3. A feeling of self-worth
4. Meaning in life (Bennion 1981, 28)

The fundamental need for acceptance by others he describes in *How Can I Help?* as the need "to give and receive love—to feel accepted by other humans, to feel care and concern from and for other humans" (Bennion 1996, 15). "Take pride in your uniqueness," he insists to each of his students in his final book (Bennion 1996, 105). He saw a harmony between the insights of psychology and humanism and the teachings of Jesus:

> Man is more than animal. His self is [only] fully realized. . . . in distinctly human endeavors. He has a mind which craves use and satisfaction. His capacity for emotional life is great. He needs to love and be loved. Man is an idealist, his eyes look to the stars. He is a dreamer, he beholds the moon. He has a memory, imagination, and the power of reason. He who would know his own worth *must live a distinctly human life, he must think, serve, imagine, belong, create, laugh and weep.* (England 1988, 244, emphasis added)

His lifelong devotion to service and his incessant call for moral responsibility on behalf of community clearly indicate he was no mere individualist, however. Human uniqueness was a gift to be given to and discovered in others, thereby inspiring a feeling that "one is contributing to life and justifying one's existence" (Bennion 1996, 105). Indeed, his understanding, drawn from the gospels and from the Book of Mormon, suggests a more moral understanding of self-worth than Maslow and other psychologists of the day offered. Self-esteem is not even an end in and itself for Bennion but a means to motivate moral concern and creativity on behalf of others. The best and highest purpose of self-expression is in service of others, not for its own sake. Creatively giving one's life to others meets that fundamental need for "the feeling or faith that life is purposeful and hence meaningful" (Bennion 1996, 15).

The great temptation he warned against throughout his life was the allure of superficial and inadequate substitutes for the deeper sense of worth that is offered by material acquisition, physical appearance, and social status: "Except for attending to basic physical comforts and reasonable beauty in our surroundings, seeking self-esteem through external means has limited value because self-esteem comes from an internal feeling and awareness" (Bennion 1996, 7). Bennion's teachings anticipated the greater troubles that have come with the onset of the internet and the smartphone: "We are too busily engaged in being entertained," he argued (Bennion 1996,

111). In a book that focuses on the ethical at greater length and that will get more attention in chapter 4, Bennion wrote, in *Do Justly and Love Mercy*, "I have often wondered if external lavishness may be a witness of the paucity within and a means of compensating for lack of internal security and satisfaction" (Bennion 1988a, 45). New Thought and Progressivism tended toward notions of the prosperity gospel, and that set off Bennion's Weberian alarms. He tempered his celebration of the individual personality and its potential by insisting that the abundant life is the domain of intentional intelligence and creativity aimed at benefiting others, not material gain.

Intelligence and Creativity

Bennion believed that Mormonism's most significant contribution to religious thought and practice was its faith in the individual's premortal and postmortal eternal journey of perpetual growth and expansion of understanding. He leveraged this confidence in the dynamic and transforming human self to mitigate religion's tendency to ossify around dogmatism and rote spirituality. As a student of religion, he understood that inertia and self-satisfaction are formidable tendencies of the religious life that must be assiduously and conscientiously defeated. "Love of knowing," he insisted, "without the love of learning, leads to dissipation of the mind" (Bennion 1996, 111).

Joseph Smith introduced a radical concept to Christianity in an 1833 revelation regarding intelligence as the eternal and coeval core of the human person: "Man was also in the beginning with God. Intelligence, or the light of truth, was not created or made, neither indeed can be. All truth is independent in that sphere in which God has placed it, to act for itself, as all intelligence also; otherwise, there is no existence" (D&C 29–30). At the outset of his career to institute students, Bennion asserts that it is "no leap into the dark to think of man—not as he now is—but of his intelligent essence as uncreated and eternal" (Bennion 1940, 48). We can also conclude, he argues, that "the free agency of man is inherent in intelligence itself" (Bennion 1940, 49) and that "man in his entirety is not wholly the creation of God" (50). Joseph Smith insisted that "intelligence" was the very "glory of God" (D&C 93:36) and the essence of "light and truth." Intelligence is, in other words, a seed within us that has always existed and that seeks to grow and increase through understanding and adherence to truth until the "perfect day" (D&C 50:24). Bennion's emphasis on the universal and inviolable power of discernment and the inherent capacity to determine value suggested original implications for the doctrine of intelligence.

Again, however, Bennion was not willing to overstate the case for human agency, which he felt would be the result of failing to acknowledge the complex web of collective agency in which an individual is caught and the contingencies of nature and environment that render certain choices possible. In his manual for institute students, we can see an early articulation of a delicate balance between the objective understanding of human behavior offered by science with the irreducible human agency found in Latter-day Saint theology:

> Man can make a choice between alternatives, more than one of which is possible. Man has *some control* over his life. It is not *wholly* the product of external forces (environment), nor is it determined *wholly* by that which the self is and has become up to the present. Man's freedom does not imply that he can do anything he wishes—ignore or "break" law or *the realities about him*. No, he must express himself, make his choices, in the real world, *among alternatives which are possible*. (Bennion 1940, 49, emphasis added)

Earlier we noted that Bennion's contemplation of the universe, in a reflection in *The Things That Matter Most*, led to the inevitable feeling that one is "powerless, expendable, contingent" (Bennion 1978, 20). As he put it simply in 1940, "man's freedom of choice is relative, not absolute" (Bennion 1940, 50). And what relativizes that freedom is everything from one's own sins or the sins of others, ignorance, injustice, and the nature of the universe itself.

Bennion's qualifications resisted a growing obsession with human freedom in the United States and in his church that was in response to the conditions of the Cold War. Anticommunist sentiment among Latter-day Saints in the post–World War II United States and during the presidency of David O. McKay ran high, and for good reason. Communism's pessimism about innate human capacity and its refusal to protect individual freedoms drove its opponents into celebrations of self-reliance and the freedom of the spirit, but these celebrations tended to focus almost exclusively on communism's evils while neglecting any critique of the pitfalls of capitalism. As a firsthand witness to the rise of Nazism in Germany, Bennion was appalled by the devastations and immorality of coercive regimes but also by the ease with which individualists surrendered responsibilities to the collective whole that enabled such power, a kind of indifference to suffering that Hannah Arendt had called the banality of evil in her 1963 study of the Holocaust (2006). The difference between freedom and enslavement, for Bennion, didn't depend as much on the structure of a particular economy as it did on the cultivation and protection of the human conscience.

Ezra Taft Benson was one of the LDS Church's most vocal anticommunists and most influential conservatives and gave voice to sentiments expressed by other Christian conservatives such as Billy Graham. In 1989, he used a memorable formulation he had developed years earlier to describe the relationship between Latter-day Saint values and social structures: "The Lord works from the inside out. The world works from the outside in. The world would take people out of the slums. Christ takes the slums out of people, and then they take themselves out of the slums. The world would mold men by changing their environment. Christ changes men, who then change their environment. The world would shape human behavior, but Christ can change human nature" (Benson 1989). Bennion endorsed the emphasis given here to the power of the individual to imagine life otherwise, but he insisted that human choices not only constitute individual behavior but shape and condition choices for others, for good and for ill. Benson's statement is a coded critique of the evils of socialism and its many offspring and a celebration of the implicit virtues of capitalism but, as such, it risks implying that the freedom of a human subject is entirely dependent on the social and economic structure of a given society, a position that would seem to contradict the inviolability of that freedom. Moreover, Benson's formulation does not address the very real possibility that capitalism could foster something just as evil as coercive socialism: the kind of coercive fascism Bennion had witnessed firsthand in Germany. Bennion's notion of freedom, contra Benson, stands in a contingent relationship to the external world of biological, social, and lived conditions that can significantly curtail that freedom and corrupt its use. The significant limitations on individual freedom that such contingencies impose can be ameliorated not through individual choice alone but also through the alleviation of those impositions by service and the creation of appropriate laws and policies.

This argument is not to suggest that Bennion didn't advocate for the principles of hard work and self-reliance; indeed, he worked for a decade with delinquent youth in Salt Lake City and formed and ran a boys' ranch for two decades for precisely that purpose. But in praising and teaching the ennobling principle of work, he never wanted his students to lose sight of the need for proper humility in the face of conditions human agency cannot control. Work, in other words, should not merely be about self-advancement or judgment of others but should be a discovery of creativity directed toward service and improvement of the conditions of others. While potentially empowering of every ounce of self-determination an individual might be able to muster, Benson's statement does not take into consideration the possibility of very real limits set by external circumstances that not only reduce but even prevent opportunities for full self-realization. And it doesn't suggest any answerability we all might have for those limits. To eschew this answerability and fetishize self-reliance risks a feedback loop where the individual is to blame for every circumstance not yet transcended by the force of the will.

Bennion agreed, but only in part, with the mantra that "as a man thinketh, so is he," the philosophy elaborated by James Allen in 1902 (Allen 2019). Bennion certainly saw an expansion of the inner life as the key to freedom but was loath to articulate any theory that could easily be used to judge or blame others for their circumstances. As he saw it, life's goal was meaning, not achievement; growth, not outcome. Meaning was found in a rich emotional, spiritual, aesthetic, intellectual, and embodied life that could find a margin of independence from, not merely as a means of controlling, circumstance. Indeed, the full phrase in Proverbs is "as a man thinketh *in his heart*, so is he." He placed his greatest hope in one's ability to give life a meaning of one's choosing that is based on how we direct our affections.

Bennion's emphasis on the intelligence of the heart is perhaps best evident in his ten aphorisms—one of his only attempts at poetry—that gained circulation among his students and the boys at his ranch and that continue to inspire young people at ranches today modeled after Bennion's life.[4] They read

> *Learn to like what doesn't cost much.*
> *Learn to like reading, conversation, music.*
> *Learn to like plain food, plain service, plain cooking.*
> *Learn to like fields, trees, brooks, hiking, rowing, climbing hills.*
> *Learn to like people, even though some of them may be different . . .*
>   *different from you.*

The Abundant Life

Learn to like to work and enjoy the satisfaction of doing your job as well as it can be done.

Learn to like the song of birds, the companionship of dogs.

Learn to like gardening, puttering around the house, and fixing things.

Learn to like the sunrise and sunset, the beating of rain on the roof and windows, and the gentle fall of snow on a winter day.

Learn to keep your wants simple and refuse to be controlled by the likes and dislikes of others. (Bennion 1996, 159)[5]

These exhortations point to the virtue of simplicity—simple living and simple pleasures—that will reduce the likelihood of our unnecessary suffering or unnecessary dependencies and increase and deepen our chances for happiness. As he concluded in his posthumous book, "Cultivate things which do not depend on money or much of it; reading, conversing, walking, visiting, listening to good music, working at inexpensive hobbies. I have always believed fervently in these words of the Savior: 'Lay up for yourselves treasures in heaven, where neither moth nor rust doth corrupt, and where thieves do not break through nor steal' (Matt. 6:20 [KJV])" (Bennion 1996, 55). Bennion saw that affections were the root of all worship, whether people end up worshiping true or false gods, and that Jesus's ministry as a teacher and shaper of the intentions and affections of the heart signaled that in affection lies the seeds of life's abundance. He did not believe this was something Christ makes happen in a vacuum, independent of our will and imagination. A creative life is a worshipful life that isn't passively shaped by society, by others, or by appetite but conforms to the highest and best aspirations cultivated in the heart with faithful and prayerful intention.

Bennion returned again and again in his writings to the idea that the purest expression of human creativity was found in "the inner life, in the realm of the mind—in thought, feeling, and imagination" (Bennion 1940, 52). Creativity, in other words, is the very seat of agency for Bennion and "satisfies our hunger and thirst for meaning" (Bennion 1996, 122). Creative self-expression can provide deep wells of self-worth: "We were born to function, to be productive, to be creative. We will not feel fulfilled unless we express ourselves in meaningful ways" (Bennion 1996, 107). To underestimate the power of one's own creativity or to squelch that power in another is to reduce a person's very humanity. As he notes in *Religion and the Pursuit of Truth*, "The search for knowledge is a great adventure consistent with man's need as a child of the great Creator to be creative. The quest for knowledge, the activity of learning, is as satisfying to the mind as is the final discovery; plowing and planting the field are as meaningful as reaping the harvest; writing a book is often more rewarding than the reading of it" (Bennion 1959, 21). In other words, to be freer from circumstances requires not merely will but a creative and imaginative inner life; it requires physical as much as mental activity—work, self-reliance, problem-solving, artistic creation, imagination, craftsmanship, and, perhaps most important, service.

Religion's tendency to produce a spirit of conformity that discourages or suppresses the creativity of the human person worried Bennion. In his concluding publication, *How Can I Help?*, he wrote, "Don't be afraid to be yourself. Listen to others, read widely, and heed counsel; but do your own thinking, draw your own conclusions, speak your own words, determine your own actions. Yes, in the process you will reveal your ignorance and make mistakes, but you will also grow, learn, and increase in integrity and self-worth. Accept full responsibility for what you feel, think, and do" (Bennion 1996, 106). He did not pretend that his church could provide a sufficient antidote to harmful environmental influences simply by announcing the doctrines of the eternal self and divine parentage, least of all when it simultaneously creates a culture of conformity that provide insufficient space for individual creativity and agency. The instinct for freely chosen creative self-expression is so strong that the individual's inner life will likely rebel at too much pressure for conformity or will create a deeply divided and unfulfilled self.

The countercultural movement of the 1960s certainly offered such a rebellion. Its unbridled celebration of self-expression would be followed by unprecedented access to affluence. In these developments, he saw the transactions of American life ironically tending toward a degradation of the individual, even as they demanded an increasingly feckless individualism as the stock in trade. A religious culture of conformity could not provide an adequate response. Bennion's defense of passionate and creative self-expression was not inspired by but was in fact aimed against the mindless individualism of contemporary US culture. As he wrote in *I Believe*, "If we would know God and progress eternally, we had best exercise our minds—read, think, talk ideas, study, and not spend our lives largely in pursuit of material or shallow things or in passive spectatorship of shallow, mindless radio programs, TV shows, movies, and books" (Bennion 1983, 49). Bennion's vision is important for a college student whose focus on education has a moral component: "Rarely have individuals had as much freedom to freely choose their careers as they have today. In taking advantage of these, few pleasures are so fulfilling as work that can make a contribution to other people and give one a sense of mastering a craft or skill" (Bennion 1996, 45). He did not want a religion content with resisting worldly trends unless it would include resistance to the feckless and rampant commercialism and materialism of US society and would inspire creative attachments to things of lasting value and proactive contributions to alleviating suffering in the world.

Creative moral action was a powerful antidote to the sexual promiscuity of US culture that had become a part of its individualism—far more effective, in his judgment, than religion's impulse to simply demand that believers curb the passions. As he suggested, "Often, if school lacks intellectual excitement or sports, hobbies, and service fail to attract a restless teen's attention, sex seems the least boring of alternative activities" (Bennion 1996, 69). He was fond of quoting the 58th section of the Doctrine and Covenants, which says that "men should be anxiously engaged in a good cause, and do many things of their own free will, and bring to pass much righteousness; For the power is in them, wherein they are agents unto themselves" (58: 27–28). Such creativity holds at bay a great many evils: "The LDS faith encourages one to participate in life to the fullest, to be anxiously engaged in good causes—in play, work, church and community service, politics, school, study, and the arts. Taboo are only those things that destroy the individual—stimulants, selfishness, infidelity, materialism" (Bennion 1983, 43). The best response to a market that knows no bounds in what it might commodify is not mere resistance or repression of appetite but an embrace of the abundance of God's gifts already available to the human spirit: "Life itself—this wonderful human existence with its marvelous capacity to see, hear, feel, laugh, weep, remember, imagine, think, love, aspire, dream, hope—is a gift. We do not have the power to create ourselves. We owe our very being to Deity and to earthly parents" (Bennion 1985a, 22).

Creative self-expression, when morally directed, becomes the best antidote to the temptations of US consumerism and its individualist extremes: "If we would preserve our individuality and cherish the feeling of living a meaningful life, we could do no better than to have faith in and cultivate our own creative nature. It is important to remember that we are an eternal self and will always live with that self. Also, each of us is a child of God and has partaken of God's creative nature. Only when we are creative can we in some way come to know and rejoice in our own souls" (Bennion 1996, 134). In this way, he offered a moral critique of society that focused less on worrying about divergent moral standards and more on the ends to which society and religion alike should be devoted: "In short, that which builds life, brings lasting and increasing joy, and helps persons to become what nature and nature's God invite them to be is good. Evil are those conditions and forces which block human growth, deny fulfillment, and impair relations among us" (Bennion 1988a, 53).

Institutional Implications

Today institutions and the aura of authority on which they often rely are increasingly seen with suspicion, particularly by the younger generations. Lowell Bennion dedicated his life to the institution of his church, to institutions of higher education, and he believed in and worked for the good that government can and should do for others. I suspect that he would be dismayed by the level of distrust for institutions that has emerged in contemporary culture, much of which is motivated by an attitude of members and citizens who have increasingly come to see themselves as consumers of the services provided by institutions but not as their cocreators. When students complained to him about problems in the church or in society, they were often met with the question, And what are you doing about it?

He understood, however, that religious institutions could not long expect to enjoy trust if they relied on what he boldly and remarkably identified for college students in *Religion and the Pursuit of Truth* as the "illegitimate children of religion": authoritarianism, institutionalism, dogmatism, and self-righteousness (Bennion 1959, 116–18). These evils result from a failure of an institution to be people-centered and explain a great deal of antireligious sentiment. Authoritarianism emerges, he explains, in political and religious contexts when "any action that is carried out" is justified "simply by reason of one's office and calling, with no regard for the value of that action in terms of religious [or moral] purpose and principle"

(116). Institutionalism similarly emerges when leaders fail to convey that an institution is not "the end and the people the means of building and supporting it" (117). Bennion understood that not all of religion's detractors should be ignored: "What men object to in the name of religion is the presentation of a creed or body of beliefs in a spirit void of humility and love, in an attitude of arrogance with the implication that religious beliefs are beyond all error, question, or thoughtful examination" (118). Institutions, in other words, cannot pretend to be above reproach or thoughtful criticism. This would be especially problematic for a religious institution that claims to ennoble "the highest ideals of religion—humility and love" (118). There is too that self-righteous tendency of believers to be drawn to institutional life "and to feel superiority to those who do not live as they do" (119). This is a kind of use of institutional loyalty that is more about tribal identity than moral responsibility and that ends up "antithetical to true religion" (119).

True religion—its most basic and simple formulations of doing justly and loving mercy—gets lost in a culture of coerced conformity. To live humbly and simply, to live with faith, to serve others with sincerity, and to love God may take a back seat to preoccupations and speculations that "lead not to edification" (119). Religion, in other words, needs to keep believers focused on the fundamentals of its very purpose, and as he demonstrated in *Religion and the Pursuit of Truth*, to do so requires a church to acknowledge the risks of institutional affiliation in its own official teachings. As we will see in the next chapter, the underlying argument of *Religion and the Pursuit of Truth* is that religion's moral purpose needs to be clearly defined and then in the minds of leaders and practitioners alike it needs to not stray from that purpose. Religion should not be an identity, and neither should it be a political ideology, or an explanatory frame that always overrides other forms of knowledge, or an excuse for any abuse of the individual person. Religious duty, in fact, includes attending to institutional health. Religion's purposes are indispensable and simple:

> [Religion is] preoccupied primarily with giving man a faith by which to live, some meaning and purpose to his existence in the universe, a way of life consistent with its purpose, and a warm fellowship in which he may work together with others to realize his faith through this worthy way of life. In these areas religion has a great contribution to make, for the things it has to offer to the human spirit are needed by men. As it

is practiced among men, however, religion is not without its evils and limitations. *One should be aware of these and seek to eradicate them, root and branch.* . . . true religion should not be condemned for men's shortcomings any more than true science should be condemned for the errors of scientists or great art for the failures of artists. (Bennion 1959, 120, emphasis added)

Jesus created a moral transformation from rules to principles and thereby invited and unleashed personal creativity in the moral life; this was the spirit that should be sustained in the Christian religious context. "The religious life," Bennion wrote in his study of the Book of Mormon, "can be much more basic, consistent, creative, free, and enjoyable if we live by principle rather than by rules or speculation" (Bennion 1985a, 35). His value-based personalism is foundational to all institutional contexts:

It is not only in government that I believe government by law or by principle is better than arbitrary personal rule. It is true in all human relationships—in church, in school, in the social group, or in the family. Human beings have free agency and, therefore, a great need of self-determination. Living by principle allows room for initiative and freedom; being under the will of another person curtails freedom and makes life insecure. Even under a benevolent dictator, one would not experience the growth that comes from self-determination. (Bennion 1985a, 111)

Any institutional tendency to curate behavior with greater and more detailed prescriptions and avoid the more sustainable and vital work of motivating righteous desires must be curtailed. The ideals of creativity and freedom for the believer should be modeled institutionally: "Religion too should be dynamic, creative, and a great adventure if it is to satisfy man's moral and spiritual aspiration" (Bennion 1959, 136).

Bennion relentlessly insisted on the religious quest as the pursuit of maximum self-realization in every aspect of personality and capacity. This meant that the sacred was never entirely apart from the secular and that education, as the means of bringing the two together, was indispensable to religion's goals. And it meant too that all church teaching and instruction should not only respect but seek to unleash the powers of creativity and agency in each human person. No human individual whose opportunities are limited or whose creativity and freedom to improvise and respond to life's circumstances are blocked can reach the potential for which God designed them. As we will explore in the subsequent chapters, religion needs to partner with the great interests of civilization that pertain to human education, health, and social and economic opportunity, and religious worship needs to focus on personal relationships and on social morality. Education and service dedicated to the full flourishing of other human beings, then, were Mormonism's claim for the means and ends of life's purpose.

CHAPTER THREE

A Rational Faith

Lowell Bennion was a beloved teacher, but his success wasn't merely because of his warm personal touch or even his emphasis on service. Easily one of his most significant theological contributions was his articulation of an integrated theology of Latter-day Saint education. He argued for a Mormonism that was broad and rational enough to be able to assimilate and respond to all forms of learning a college student might encounter and the many contradictions experienced in the modern world. Sympathetic to the argument of J. B. Phillips's 1953 book (republished in 2004), *Your God Is Too Small*, he believed it a religious failure to imagine that faith was not capacious enough to accommodate the concerns and challenges faced in modern life. A rational faith for Bennion meant a form of Mormonism, in other words, that did not beat a retreat from secular learning but could catalyze an adventurous and fulfilling faith that was loyal to God and responsive to life itself.

Ways of Knowing Divine Truth

Bennion's strongest articulations of a resilient and holistic Latter-day Saint theology of education is evident in a manual for general members, *An Introduction to the Gospel* (1955), and in two manuals for college students, *The Religion of the Latter-day Saints* (1940) and *Religion and the Pursuit of Truth* (1959). In each of these books, the word of God, as presented in scripture and occasionally as taught authoritatively by the highest levels of church leadership, was his primary and foundational source to identify the larger and more unified understanding he sought. But, of course, any reading of the word involves interpretation, and therefore he offered a robust theology of education to confront the problem of hermeneutics and epistemology. In *Religion and the Pursuit of Truth*, Bennion offered a provocatively, even if perhaps overly, simple formula for understanding how we come to know the world. Although it doesn't include a sense of human psychology and of what today is known as motivated reasoning, his formula does effectively stress individual responsibility for knowing: "One gains knowledge in four ways: (1) by accepting it on the authority of someone else, (2) by thinking, (3) by experiencing, (4) and by feeling which may be called intuition, mysticism, inspiration, or revelation" (1959, 24). A faith that would consistently incorporate these different ways of gaining knowledge over time was for Bennion a preferable and more rational faith than one that relied on only one method.

Because of the Latter-day Saint belief in modern prophets and modern revelation, the question of authority has remained somewhat of a Gordian Knot for members and church leaders alike. The LDS Church has never taught that prophets are infallible, even if it has repeatedly insisted on the central importance and exceptional nature of its leaders' authority and the unquestionable need for members to follow prophetic counsel. As a result, Latter-day Saints tend to implicitly, if not explicitly, defend a particular definition of infallibility that rests on the idea that the prophet will never lead the church astray, which has been interpreted by some to mean that when the prophet has spoken, the debate is over.[1] Blanket trust of this kind was worrisome to Bennion and to anyone else, including church leaders, who prized individual conscience and wanted to protect and encourage individual accountability for belief. But how to do so while duly recognizing and honoring the sacred nature of apostolic leadership has remained a challenge. If truth should be at the service of moral behavior, obtaining a knowledge of the truth secondhand robs an individual of the growth and development that can come from individual striving. Since this is counterproductive to the gospel's aim of self-realization, blind trust puts knowledge to bad use, even if that knowledge is otherwise true.

For this very reason, Bennion was quick to point out that church leaders "would not have us believe that every sentence they have ever uttered was the word of God to us" (Bennion 1959, 146). Because of the LDS Church's understandable need to stress the more important issue of continuity of authority and to inspire institutional confidence, disagreements among contemporary leaders or over time have usually been played down or ignored altogether by the institution in its official presentations of its teachings. Inspired by his experiences in Europe just as Nazism was on the rise, Bennion contextualized the question of authority more broadly beyond church life to help his readers see the common sense of his argument: "in every walk of life [men and women] have been known to err" and that "authorities, even on the same subject, often contradict each other" (1959, 25, 26). In today's age, where cable news pundits, talk radio hosts, social media, and Hollywood stars have been granted far more authority than they merit and the power and importance of individual reason have been undermined, Bennion's words seem prescient.

Bennion's acknowledgment of the inevitability of contradiction and fallibility was not intended to disparage the authority of church leaders but to teach students why their own agency mattered and what, ultimately, trust and loyalty could look like in a rational faith. He taught that, because trust in authority is "often geared to the past[, it] does not lend itself to correction and enlargement by the experience of those who come on the scene at a later date" (1959, 26). Ultimately, what is at stake is the ever-important ability of the individual to discern good leaders and know why and when one chooses to trust their authority. Such ability is vital to self-realization:

> People who accept the truth simply on the authority of others are prone to shift full responsibility to such authority for their own thought and behavior. . . . Blind, submissive followers in any field, be it in government, science, or religion, lack the ability to discriminate between truth and error, good and evil, and between the weightier and lesser matters of the law. They hardly have a soul of their own. This kind of discipleship is not befitting a Latter-day Saint. He believes in giving loyalty and respect to political and religious authority; but at the same time, as a child of God endowed with free agency and the Holy Ghost, he senses his responsibility to be a thoughtful and whole-souled disciple of Jesus Christ. He will follow those who have earned the right to be his leaders. And he will follow them with understanding and conviction, not with blindness or indifference. (Bennion 1959, 27)

He sought a formula for establishing trust that ennobles, rather than diminishes, the soul and is the same for establishing trust in one's own spiritual impressions: "We shall always need authorities to guide us, but we must learn to test their right to lead us. This we can do through thought, experience, and revelation" (1959, 29).

In his own relationship with President David O. McKay, Bennion applied these principles. He had tremendous admiration for President McKay. In him, he saw a fellow lover of the arts and ideas, a compassionate personality, and a kindred spirit. He trusted in his prophetic authority and he pledged his loyalty to him, but he understood from McKay himself that loyalty did not require an abdication of conscience or a premature resolution of contradiction in one's conscience or in one's ideas. As mentioned in chapter 1, when McKay first hired Bennion at the institute, McKay instructed him with wise counsel, wisdom that Bennion would frequently teach to others: "Be true to yourself and loyal to the cause; and if you are, feel free to draw upon your best thinking and experience from any source" (1988a, 89–90). He wrote, fifteen years after McKay's death, "It is fitting that we are reminded to give heed to our leaders. They are not perfect in character nor in judgment. They err on occasion. They should be and are open to suggestion and question, but they have been chosen prayerfully and generally give their best efforts freely. They merit our support, all the more because we have raised our hands to sustain them" (1985a, 46). His dedication to this formula is perhaps why Bennion could appreciate and follow the many teachings McKay offered and see the good fruit it yielded while also having the confidence to speak privately with McKay to ask pointed questions about the priesthood ban.

He saw a corollary in members' relationship with the scriptures. The scriptures too should be trusted and should be central to one's moral worldview, but because their meaning is not self-evident, any scriptural understanding also needed to be checked against reason, experience, and other scriptures. This led Bennion to conclude that "No passage of scripture should be interpreted and accepted at face value if it denies God's love and justice and (or) the free agency and dignity of man" (1959, 167). In 1983, he remained committed to the same approach, elaborating on it in a way that reflects his personalism: "I refuse to accept any interpretation of scripture or of the gospel that contradicts or impedes the free agency of man and his brotherhood with all men, *or that bars his opportunity for self-realization*" (1983, 80, emphasis added).

Revelation, in other words, requires constant study, experimentation, and discernment because its meaning and content are never fully self-evident.

Whether it comes to an individual personally or through prophetic mediums in scripture or in the living church, revelation is God's character and will, refracted and reframed through the language and mundane circumstances of particular human contexts. It is, for Bennion, a real phenomenon and one to be treasured in the religious life, but it results from work, specifically the work of translation between the mind and will of God and limited human understanding. The content of the revelation is always understood in the context of human language, culture, and even personal history, and its most important message is love: "It seems to me that revelation always has two parts—the content of the revelation itself and the indescribably uplifting love manifested in God's willingness to communicate with us" (1985a, 101). As a result, loyalty to revelation begins with a determination to reciprocate that love, a motivation that will maximize revelation's potential to facilitate moral growth. Blind devotion is not love, since it does not require discernment. Because revelation is always only a partial disclosure of the truth, it therefore must be continually searched and continually given if it is going to be revelation at all. Interpretation of revelation must be inspired by the same spirit that brought it: "by humility, . . . a contrite heart, . . . a devotional and reverent spirit, seeking the guidance of the Holy Spirit" (1959, 171). Armed with such principles, a reader could more safely test a given revelation against the whole of revelation, against reason, and against life itself, against what one sees and understands from one's own observations. In this continual testing and probing, continual revelation becomes possible.

The signature scripture Bennion most frequently used to teach the principle of revelation as continual translation is found in the first section of the Doctrine and Covenants, which reads:

> Behold, I am God and have spoken it; these commandments are of me, and were given unto my servants in their weakness, after the manner of their language, that they might come to understanding. And inasmuch as they erred it might be made known; And inasmuch as they sought wisdom they might be instructed; And inasmuch as they sinned they might be chastened, that they might repent; And inasmuch as they were humble they might be made strong, and blessed from on high, and receive knowledge from time to time. (D&C 1:24–28)

Bennion read these verses as a confirmation that "scriptures are inspired of God, but are given in man's language and according to his circumstances

A Rational Faith

and need" (1959, 158). It is necessary to apprehend both the divine and human elements of scripture in order to avoid attributing to God what human beings have mistakenly believed:

> Scriptures reflect both God and man. When we find teachings or interpretations of history therein which are wholly inconsistent with the character and purposes of God as revealed to Jesus Christ or to the prophets, then we should look for an explanation in men—either in the writers, copyists, translators, the people for whom they were intended, or in our own lack of understanding as readers. (Bennion 1959, 162)

Bennion was, then, loyal to revelation but not without full use of his reasoning and his need to test it against the whole of scriptural wisdom and experience. He was not interested in using reason to debunk revelation or to deconstruct scripture, nor for that matter was he willing to blindly accept traditional interpretations of revelation and thereby allow false understandings to persist. His goal was to protect the sacred stature of scripture and of prophetic teachings from the conclusion that, once tainted by inevitable human interest or bias, revelation was nothing more than delusion. He also wanted to use the process of continual revelation and a balanced method of corroboration to filter out elements that distorted human understanding of God's wisdom.

Ever since the event that is known in Mormonism as Joseph Smith's First Vision in a grove of trees in Palmyra, New York, personal revelation has been a cornerstone of Latter-day Saint theology and practice. Nevertheless, Bennion would insist that to uphold the special status of revelation as above human limitations was to contradict its personal nature and set it up for failure. "Personal revelation," in other words, is a concept that embodies a paradox. He cited Brigham Young, who insisted that it was "impossible" for human beings "to receive a revelation from the Almighty in all its perfection. He has to speak to us in a manner to meet the extent of our capacities" (Bennion 1959, 163). Personal revelation, then, is both transcendent of and embedded in the contingent and therefore it must be continual: "To me, it seems far more in keeping with God's continuing concern for us that, as Alma testifies, God inspires men and women of all nations and in all ages with his word to the degree they desire and are able to understand. It is consistent with his fatherhood and justice and with his goals regarding human life" (1985a, 31). Assessing the human ingredient of revelation allows one to discern a fuller measure of what has been divinely given and yet still remain open to further revelation. Bennion advocated love as the key to this hermeneutics: "If everything in the law and the prophets hangs on love, then love must be used as the basis of scriptural interpretation" (1988a, 9). A hermeneutics of suspicion aimed at scripture results in cynicism, while a hermeneutics of suspicion aimed at "the world" results in an unexamined defensiveness about the always exceptional and transcendent status of revelation: "The scriptures are not perfect, but their virtues and values far outweigh their defects and limitations. They should be read in proper perspective just for what they are—neither with blind devotion, now with the cynic's eye" (Bennion 1959, 176–77). Bennion's elaboration of this hermeneutics, it should be noted, is remarkably consistent with Alan Jacobs's theory in *A Theology of Reading* (2001) and the work of Paul Ricoeur (for example, 1980), and strikes a unique balance between the extremes of poststructuralist and fundamentalist readings.

In this way, the human element of revelation does not pose a dilemma, but it offers grounds for hope.[2] In Bennion's formulation, what breaks human understanding out of the potential cycle of making the same errors perpetually and makes new revelations and understandings possible is a combination of open-minded curiosity, trust and love, and measured reason and circumspection that prize wisdom over knowledge and moral growth over certitude:

> Revelation, like intuition, is a private communication. How can we decide between the claims of Micah and the popular prophets whom he condemned? Their respective teachings must be tested by reason, by experience, and by the witness of Deity to us. In fact, all knowledge-claims based on intuition or revelation need to be tested by reason, by experience, and by other revelations which we have come to trust. And they need also to be tested by our own intuition and by confirmation of the Spirit to us. (Bennion 1959, 38)

As discussed in chapter 1, the priesthood ban of men of African descent clearly failed this test for Bennion. Its many offensive justifications were examples of the danger of failing to admit the human dimension in revelation and failing to judge an assertion against the collective wisdom of scripture and of experience. His intention was not to offer a model of revelation that would decrease faith in and loyalty to church leaders but would rather inspire a more resilient and sustainable loyalty to a fallible but inspired institution with fallible but inspired leaders who he believed were divinely charged to deliver revealed truth to humankind. He firmly held that, if revelation is seen as ongoing, partial, and never final, believers will take more responsibility for it and seek further refinement and deeper humility for greater access to the mind and will of God.

Of course, even determining God's character is a fraught hermeneutical question. Clearly, Bennion could be guilty of borrowing from secular logic or liberal political discourse to color his own beliefs about God's moral nature. Nor did he seem bothered by the fact that there was no escaping the risks of interpretation and the inevitability of bias. Indeed, that fact was why it is necessary to be conscious and deliberate and judicious in how and why one interprets as one does. He advocated a principled approach to hermeneutics by studying closely the life of Jesus: "The student should keep in mind that it is from Jesus that we gain our highest concept of the character and will of our Heavenly Father" (Bennion 1959, 169). Determining the character and will of God, in any case, is not as complicated as it might seem: "To help me know the will of God, I trust above all others the teachings, the Spirit, and the example of Jesus. I trust the great fundamentals of religion repeated and illustrated again and again by Amos, Micah, Jeremiah, Alma, Paul, and living prophets. I also seek the confirmation of the Spirit and of my own observation and experience" (1985a, 13). He was particularly fond of the verse from Nephi that reads "I know that [God] loveth his children; nevertheless I do not know the meaning of all things" (1 Nephi 11:17). Trust in God's love gave him confidence in the journey of faith: "To know what is just and true is to grow in knowledge of God. When the quest for justice and truth becomes painful and hard, I am sustained in knowing that Jesus said, 'Come unto me, all ye that labour and are heavy laden, and I will give you rest' [Matt. 11:28]" (1985a, 13).

A religious passion for divine truth that is grounded in impatience or excessive trust in one's own understandings not only distorts the truth but potentially warps character. Believers, in other words, are often tempted to confuse their trust in God with confidence in their own limited understanding of His will and thus use the gospel as a weapon to fight life's battles. Such a method of discernment (or actually lack of it) is really a form of idol worship for Bennion, a way of using belief in God's truth to serve human and selfish ends: "Let us not restrict the Lord in his creation to our limited knowledge and perspective," he exhorts. "Let him move and act in his realm from his perspective of which we know relatively little" (1985a, 34). The aim of gospel truths is to enable and further the development of human character and self-realization as children of God, which only happens if believers learn sufficient humility to purify their own motives: "'To action alone hast thou a right, not to fruits.' We have only limited control over the fruit of our actions. Man proposes, life disposes. . . . I am learning to put my heart and mind into what I am doing and to not work for success or rewards. In this way, I am not serving two masters. I am not working to be seen of men but for its own sake" (1985a, 31).

His understanding of the process of revelation becomes an argument, as we will see, for a strong focus on the moral and ethical priorities of the gospel to build a good life for oneself and others. Such a focus stimulates a rational faith that can distinguish between "the things that matter most" and the things that are "irrelevant to religious living here and now" (1985a, 35). Moral focus on doing good to help others to flourish provides self-satisfaction and protects against undue pressure and anxiety about always needing to have certainty about what is true: "Alma promises that if we will exercise faith and live the teachings of the gospel of Jesus Christ, we shall find peace and joy in our living. We shall not be frustrated or forever restless and dissatisfied. Life will have meaning, strength, and deep satisfaction" (1985a, 70). A moral focus means that the work of education and the shaping of the mind is collective and outward-oriented and the self is invested in a cooperation and an integration of the sacred and the secular toward common goals for the entire human family. Truth, in other words, is not a prize believers win and possess. Its relentless pursuit is what inspires moral growth toward the character of Jesus.

Religion and the Pursuit of Truth

In order to meet the individual's need for full self-realization, religious education must provide an introduction to the fundamental doctrines of Christ's gospel, but it must also appeal to the intellectual, social, moral, and spiritual development of the whole student. It cannot afford the risks of compartmentalization. "The mind," Bennion insisted, "is a single dwelling, not a duplex or an apartment house. It craves unity and wholeness" (1996, 8). He worried that if students failed to see the relevance of their religion to the riddles and struggles of contemporary society and to their own very personal and pressing concerns, they might leave it behind. His emphasis on student-centered learning meant not only that teaching and moral formation should be centered on loving relationships, as we explored in chapter 2, but on the premise that spiritual ideals must be made answerable to the historical and social moment of the student. He urged this responsibility onto his students: "Not only must the student correlate his university studies with one another," he wrote, "but also with his total life's experience, including his religion" (1959, 3).

The Latter-day Saint struggle for much of the twentieth century and to this day has been how and where to create the space to correlate in this way. LDS Church services could provide some opportunities, but those opportunities are challenged by the fact that people of all educational levels and dispositions congregate at church where worship is the primary objective and by the fact that, after the 1960s, the LDS Church adopted an approach to its curriculum, known as correlation even though it achieved a very different kind of correlation. Indeed, it rendered church manuals increasingly detached from important intellectual questions and the total life experience of members. In response to this approach, following the spirit of the Swearing Elders, members created such journals as *Dialogue* (founded by Bennion's student Eugene England and others) and *Sunstone* in the 1960s and 1970s and various independent presses. Later in the 1990s and beyond, members proliferated digital resources in blogs, podcasts, and websites, dedicated to intellectual and theological questions across the political and religious spectrums. This significant proliferation and diversification of Latter-day Saint discourse more freely and independently developed has only increased in recent years, resulting in many creative articulations of faithful paths that LDS intellectuals might take. As noted earlier, the LDS Church has needed and benefited from these efforts, as it did from Bennion's, even if it has not always been able or willing to officially sponsor them. Formal church correlation, in other words, has not led to the kind of correlation and integration Bennion advocated and has instead inspired supplementary sources that meet with support or suspicion or both, resulting in an ambivalence that stalls consensus.

Institutes and other ancillary religious education offerings were, in Bennion's view, the ideal space to address the needs of the whole person, and they remain today a potentially viable space. When religious education in these contexts remains compartmentalized and isolated from, or even hostile to, the larger concerns and issues students confront in higher education and in society, it has tended to sell religion short, even in an effort to protect it. The ability to correlate and synthesize learning within the framework of faith is vital to the long-term viability of belief in the lifespan of one person: "religion must make peace with a man's total life experience if it is to retain a wholesome place in his living and thinking" (Bennion 1959, 8). Or again: "Religion embraces the whole of life and seeks a meaning in it" (Bennion 1959, 90). If the default assumption is that religion is either irrelevant or antagonistic to "the world" of contemporary living and thinking, religion risks becoming diminished in its power.

Therefore, Bennion took pains in his manuals not just to present doctrine but to argue for a rational faith relevant to all forms of knowing. In *An Introduction to the Gospel*, he explains that to even present a "systematic study of the doctrines or beliefs of a church [that] is called *theology*" and that "It is important also in our study of theology to try to see things as a whole, various ideas in relationship to one another. . . . Our search in this study will be for a whole view of life—for an understanding of God, man, and Christ in their relationship to one another" (Bennion 1955, 3–4). Religious instruction in doctrine, in other words, is never theologically neutral but is inherently an exercise in interpretation and therefore an exercise in theology itself. Church correlation of manuals, by contrast, implies that doctrinal understandings are self-evident, often without showing the interpretive work that generates lesson manuals in the first place. This state of affairs risks two consequences. First, theology can become a terrain of benign neglect, if not suspicion, in the LDS Church. And, second, without providing instruction about how and why to interpret scriptures and without any reference to contemporary life, the manuals that correlation has produced can create the appearance that church teachings so utterly transcend lived experience that readers' own powers of interpretation are unnecessary. Excessive deference to authority and a denigration of the power and responsibility of individual interpretation can result.

Although he believed religion was central to the quest of education, Bennion also affirmed that religion should not overstep its bounds. Like other religious modernists, he believed that religion should be receptive to all truth, that it should not believe itself already and always adequately providing all answers about the entirety of reality. Its high purpose is to

66

point the way to a meaningful and moral life. To do so, it must be responsive to both faith and reason. "Religion," he wrote, "is more than feeling, more than hope, more than mystery. It also includes moral precepts and theological postulates that provide thoughtful perspectives on significant areas of life. The religious life should be motivated by faith, but also be guided by the logic of the gospel as well as by the Spirit. I believe that impressions of the Spirit should be checked by the logic of gospel fundamentals even as I believe we should pray concerning our rational conclusions" (Bennion 1983, 81). His bold vision of the inherent reasonableness of Latter-day Saint belief and its total reach into the whole of life meant that, by definition and perhaps paradoxically, it would sometimes need to be a receptacle rather than a source of truth. It could, however, remain the source of moral principle that guides the use of knowledge in an integrated and moral life:

> Religion does not give us a complete view of life unless, like Mormonism, it is free to embrace truth from all sources. . . . Religion needs the fruit of science, art, philosophy, and rich everyday living to fulfill itself in the life of man; and men of religion have often had the wisdom to employ the knowledge and inspiration available in these other fields. . . . If religion included all truth, beauty, and goodness, there would be no need to seek after these things in other places. Since it does not, however, we also look to science, the arts, philosophy, and everyday life for a larger understanding of life which we can use to realize the values and purposes postulated by our religious faith. (Bennion 1959, 114–15)

This was a particularly Latter-day Saint principle, as he saw it. He insisted that one of the central messages of his church's keystone text, the Book of Mormon, was that "no religious group, not even the Church of Jesus Christ, has a monopoly on truth and goodness" (1985a, 30).

Bennion clearly shared Brigham Young's vision of Mormonism as a never-ceasing quest for the integration of all truth, one that has inspired Latter-day Saint educational aspirations since the beginning.[3] Claiming itself to contain both the restoration of ancient truths and continual revelation, Mormonism is both a triumphant claim on divine revelation and a bold admission of the limits of human understanding and the need to gather further knowledge:

> The Gospel of Jesus Christ is authoritative. It would teach men truths of eternal validity and universal application. Yet, it is not a closed book, a

finished system of thought, the last word of God to man; for it is based on a principle of growth—continuous revelation—on the faith that God has, does now, and will yet reveal His will to men. *The very content of religion, itself, will therefore, increase and be enlarged.* Man may search for truth in religion, as elsewhere, eternally! Each individual, each generation, must appropriate anew, truths discovered and revealed by men who have gone before. So regardless of how much religious truth has been made known; yes, even though the Gospel of Jesus Christ has been revealed in its fullness in relation to that which has gone before, to each one of us remains the task and challenge to understand and live it. (1940, 21, emphasis added)

Latter-day Saints, then, cannot afford to be complacent, either about what has already been revealed or known or what might still be to come, from whatever source: "We think of God as the embodiment and great source of truth. We consider religion as an all-inclusive way of life. *Any quest for truth then, is, in a sense, a religion quest*" (1940, 20, emphasis added). To be religious, then, means to be seeking new knowledge as well as to be making the past one's own. Legacies and inheritances of knowledge are not to be protected and cherished but earned anew through individual rigorous study and reception. As he was fond of quoting from Goethe's *Faust*: "What from your father's heritage is lent, / Earn it anew to really possess it" (Bennion 1940, 287). "In studying the scriptures," he further insisted, "the student should strive to make them his very own" (Bennion 1959, 178).

The interesting paradox he espouses here is that Mormonism cannot claim to be universal if it claims to already contain all truth; its ability to encompass all of life depends on its ability to welcome and integrate other forms of knowledge. The key was to use religion as a broad enough context to allow space for sometimes competing or even contradictory forms of knowledge to continue to germinate. Whenever contradiction emerges between different fields of knowledge, a faithful path forward is possible:

(1) if the student will let art be art, science be science, philosophy be philosophy, and religion be religion; if he will not confuse their roles in life but will let each serve life in its own way; (2) if he will follow the wisdom of Aristotle's thought, "It is the mark of an educated mind to be able to entertain a thought without accepting it" (or rejecting it, one might add);

(3) and if he will—be he student of science, philosophy, or religion—learn humility and remain teachable through the various avenues of learning which the Creator has made available to men. (Bennion 1959, 52)

The gospel, in other words, should be big enough to provide a context into which believers can assimilate different ways of knowing without becoming indifferent or unnecessarily antagonistic. Students will prematurely dismiss religion if it has not had an adequate chance to square with lived experience, especially if religion is not satisfactorily presented as relevant to the whole of life and if students can't see how its principles saturate every dimension of life. So, while he worried about dogmatism and zealotry, he believed in a truly passionate religious impulse that should inspire lifelong seriousness about all forms of learning.

Weber made a distinction between the functions of empirical knowledge and value-based understandings (1949). Bennion similarly explains in *Religion and the Pursuit of Truth* that education presents a student with different "provinces" of various ways of knowing the world, each of which adds a vital component of understanding in the pursuit of truth that should be welcomed, not shunned: "No single avenue of knowledge has given us the whole truth about life. No single approach to truth can stand alone. We need them all to supplement one another and to verify one another as much as it is possible for them to do" (Bennion 1959, 38). Science, for example, is "not normative but only descriptive" and the province of religion, by the same token, pertains to moral behavior more than to descriptions of how the world works (68). Among those provinces, Latter-day Saint intellectual endeavors should be characterized by the spirit of gathering, not by the metaphor of trench warfare. Excessive confidence in the epistemological reach of any one epistemology can run certain risks and become self-defeating: "The tragedy begins when a person with a single view tries to explain the whole of reality from such a narrow base" (41). To make this mistake is to fail to use faith, a necessary dimension of all knowledge: "there is no genuine faith without some knowledge. However, knowledge, by its very nature, is limited. Any quest for it is a venture in faith. Any acquirement of it only makes one aware of his need for more faith" (184). Ultimately, the faith that suffers contradiction also hopes to encompass and integrate: "If a marriage is to be consummated between reason and faith, it will have to be of the same kind we know between husband and wife—one that respects individuality in their respective natures and roles. The concern here is not to achieve identity, nor even complete harmony, but rather a working relationship which will ensure a rich, constructive life" (1959, foreword).

Bennion urged his readers to be patient with contradiction and not to force a reconciliation, since that might lead to either willed ignorance of secular truths or disillusionment with religion. The proper balance was faithfulness to what one knows, especially "the weightier matters" of a moral life identified by Old Testament prophets and an openness to what is yet to be understood, including corrections of one's past understanding. He wrote, "Let us distinguish between what is important and not important and live by the great fundamentals of faith and righteousness" (1985a, 36). To remain open to new knowledge perpetually requires "an attitude of open-mindedness, a childlike curiosity about things, a search for knowledge and understanding" (Bennion 1955, 1).

Thought mattered to Bennion, but as we will see in chapter 4, it mattered for how it could facilitate better moral action in the world. Religious and secular thought are both impoverished by a misplaced obsession with identity and with "being right." Here was the wisdom, as he saw it, of the modernist emphasis on ethics; it could keep religion from an obsession with right belief and help it to remain focused on the realization of the flourishing moral self. Ethics was not just necessary to religion but to secular education as well. When knowledge is segregated from aesthetic experience, human relationships, wonder at nature, creative expression, or from the social and political work of building a better society, it becomes self-serving and loses its moral potential. In an especially insightful passage, he argues that faith is an awareness of the incompleteness of human knowledge that propels growth:

> Faith is adventurous and creative. . . . Faith is that remarkable quality of the human spirit which first envisages the possibilities of life, the lives as though these possibilities were realities, and by this action often makes them real. In the realm of knowledge, one conforms to what is; in the realm of faith, one creates life after the image carried in his heart. Faith adds another dimension to life. Recognizing the borders of knowledge, it transcends them. (Bennion 1959, 125–26)

In other words, "we should aim to harmonize these various avenues to truth, not so much with each other as in life as a whole" (Bennion 1955,

16). It follows that a deliberate life of values helps to guide conceptual work toward moral ends.

Religion finds its relevance to the whole of life when faith acts like "a searchlight which takes us beyond the boundaries of knowledge" (1985a, 69). Faith that understands itself as a journey, not as a destination, becomes "creative, futuristic, dynamic, adventurous," and the believer is instructed by revelation and by experience both. As he put it in *Religion and the Pursuit of Truth,*

> Art, science, philosophy, and religion have grown out of man's daily needs. Their great value lies in their ability to help him interpret and fulfil his full nature as a human being. Everyday living is both the main source and the chief end of these specialized approaches to life. Everyday life needs the guidance of the specialist; but the specialist should not overlook the insights and wisdom of the common man. (Bennion 1959, 101)

When religion seems primarily aimed at its own perpetuation and fails to call believers to a lifelong high moral purpose in the service of everyday life, it will, he feared, inspire boredom and malaise and increase the likelihood of faith crises among the young.

He saw that believers too easily come to think of faith as a series of conclusions about reality, but he stressed that faith is really a form of trust in a higher and more integrated reality and makes an insistent claim, therefore, that one's understanding of that reality is always limited. If faith cannot acknowledge or tolerate the gap between what is known and what is knowable, temptation will likely follow. Acknowledging ignorance, on the other hand, relieves us of the burden of overreach: "I found it a great relief to know what I know, but to recognize unashamedly what I don't know" (1985a, 40).

In a lay church where official catechisms are largely absent and folk theology abounds, there is the risk of lazy thinking or excessive deference to authority or both. He chose instead to emphasize the opportunity Mormonism created not just to be loyal to what one knows but also to be simultaneously in constant pursuit of higher and better understanding. Faith, for Bennion, should never justify lazy rejection or equally lazy self-satisfaction: "To discard one's religious faith because one has studied and practiced it earnestly and found it wanting is understandable; but to give it up because of sheer neglect is the height of folly" (Bennion 1959, 10).

For that matter, "Religion," he insists, "deserves our best thinking. We are to love the Lord our God with all our minds as well as with all our hearts" (1988a, 90). To accept things by faith does not circumvent the need for serious and careful study: "As we study the religion of the LDS Church of Jesus Christ of Latter-day Saints, let us do so critically with all our powers of mind at work. Let us also, however, study in a spirit of humility with our hearts tuned to God, that through his inspiration we may know the falseness or truth of the ideas presented to us" (Bennion 1955, 1). He challenges his students to be deliberate and thoughtful about their faith: "How much time do you now devote to (a) thinking about the Gospel or religious history, (b) church activity? How does your knowledge of religion compare with your knowledge in your major subject? What bearing does religion have on your present everyday decisions and reflections on life's goals or values?" (Bennion 1940, 14).

Bennion saw a tendency among his students to prize feeling, intuition, or "impressions" as a unique path to spiritual knowledge. While he understood the value of such experiences, he worried that such a rarified or narrow path to spiritual truth risks ignoring reason, the fundamental principles of the gospel, or direct experience and could risk the eventual collapse of religious faith in the face of life (Bennion 1959, 38). "Knowledge," he explained, "which appeals to our minds, warms our hearts, is verified in experience and is attested to by trustworthy witnesses in their respective fields, is most certainly part of the truth we seek" (38). The fervent prayer seeking confirmation of eternal truth offered by a supplicant uninterested or uninvested in the quest for an adventurous moral life would not do. The advantage of a moral emphasis, as we will explore more in chapter 4, relieves the individual of considerable and sometimes unnecessary cognitive burdens, even if it places greater emphasis on action. It also opens more avenues for confirming truth. Bennion would often point to the simple fact that loving and serving others, as Jesus did, can lift one's own spirits and bring deep satisfaction to the soul, or that repentance and humility bring deeper levels of joy. The gospel truths, in other words, were more relevant to empirical experience and available to reasoned experimentation than at first glance. Placing belief too far out of reach of direct experience or of moral relevance—leaving it merely to the conceptual or emotional realm of human experience—risks making it more vulnerable to collapse. Attending to the weightier matters of moral reformation and human flourishing allows space and time for doubts and questions on lesser matters of belief to resolve themselves or at least to find a healthier place in a more balanced life.

Even knowledge of salvific truth needs room for growth: "To know in one's heart by the witness of the Spirit that God lives does not mean that one knows all there is to know about God" (Bennion 1959, 63). Bennion would insist that the kind of sure knowledge Latter-day Saints describe as "testimony" was not an end or a reward but a means to a fuller realization of human potential:

> Theology rests ultimately on faith in the revelations of God, but the ethical aspects of religion are tested constantly in everyday living. . . . We may maintain that we know by the Spirit that our theology is true. I respect this kind of personal witness. But we can also know the truth of repentance, humility, and love by the same Spirit and, in addition, can see and experience their fruits. (1988a, 8)

As he then added, "Theological differences divide people; whereas, justice and mercy tend to unite them. . . . Justice and mercy must speak louder than theological beliefs" (1988a, 9). To care more about salvation than service or to care more about belief than moral action was to misunderstand the very foundations of divinely appointed human purpose. Bennion certainly believed in the importance of distinguishing truth from error, but if believers weren't also instructed on the perils of erroneous judgment, religion might end up overpromising what believers can know.

The power of religion stems from its capacity to place intellectual conceits or the conceptual work of belief at the service of moral development. Thinking matters but never for its own sake. The gospel of Jesus Christ provided a moral context into which knowledge could be received, charging believers to identify ways in which knowledge could be used for the purpose of the betterment of humankind. While judgment discerns whether an idea is true or false, a moral motivation more appropriately determines whether knowledge will be good or bad. He reminded his students that

> Every Latter-day Saint should serve his community as well as his church. . . . If we are to help solve the problems of mankind, we must prepare ourselves both spiritually through prayer and gospel study and also intellectually by reading and studying out of the best books. The problems we face are exceedingly complex, requiring not only the ideals of the

gospel, but also a realistic knowledge of economic, political, legal, and behavioral principles. The world needs desperately . . . professionals who combine pragmatic knowledge with Christian idealism" (England 1988, 266–67).

The pursuit of knowledge, then, presents moral opportunities and challenges similar to the pursuit of material wealth. Education can and will canker the soul and diminish opportunities for others if it is not put to moral use. Our ability to gather, correlate, and consecrate knowledge depends on whether its pursuit is motivated by our love of God and of our fellow beings or by pride and arrogance. So, Bennion wanted students, before they ventured into the disputes between, say, science and religion or religion and philosophy, to obtain a moral motivation behind the acquisition of knowledge, so that they would be less distracted by controversies and more responsive to the service to which God calls them.

Institutional Implications

Lowell Bennion championed and systematized the ideals and ambitions of a Latter-day Saint education that had been first articulated by Joseph Smith and Brigham Young and that had been refined by early-twentieth-century church leaders. By the late 1930s, he was formally positioned to produce this work and was coming into his own intellectually just as the institutional fervor for higher education that had drawn him and others to top-flight graduate programs began to wane. As discussed in chapter 1, Elder J. Reuben Clark's address in 1938, "The Charted Course of the LDS Church in Education," provided an authoritative statement of suspicion toward secular learning that continued to influence Latter-day Saint academic culture (Clark 1938). Consequently, Bennion's work made important inroads even as it was perpetually met with an ambivalence that welcomed and yet hesitated to fully embrace his vision.

A noteworthy legacy of this era and of Bennion's strong advocacy is that the various private universities of the Church of Jesus Christ of Latter-day Saints remain among the few universities left in the United States that espouse simultaneously serious secular learning and academic achievement with serious commitment to spiritual meaning and moral growth. Indeed, he was hired and his manuals were published precisely because the LDS church was firm in its commitment to education. Today, wherever LDS students find themselves at other universities, LDS Institutes of Religion provide supplementary classes to perform the kind of integrating work that Bennion started at the University of Utah. Bennion's formula for an adventurous faith that welcomes the challenge and opportunity for faith to inform and to be informed by all forms of learning resonated with many Latter-day Saints, including many educational and ecclesiastical leaders, and remains a lasting invitation to young and old alike to be religiously serious about education.

What is less clear, however, is how successful that integration has been. As younger generations of Latter-day Saints have grown less invested in settling truth claims, less trustful of institutions, and more attuned to peer chatter on social media, the LDS Church has encountered new challenges, as have all other sects in America even if to a lesser degree, in keeping young people engaged and invested in religious practice.[4] Moreover, despite the overt intention for a full integration of faith and learning in these vari-ous institutional contexts, a persistent ambivalence about the prospects of such an integration often keeps them separate. The result is a sometimes bifurcated ambition for Latter-day Saint students to excel academically but to be less interested in or aware of the intellectual, ethical, and theological implications of or motivations for their achievements.

In 1986, Elder Boyd K. Packer offered an approach to religious education that resurrected J. Reuben Clark Jr.'s charted course for church education from 1938 and that has predominated in church manuals, institutes, and equivalent courses in high school, known to Latter-day Saints as semi-nary. Packer's vision is a notable departure from the direction Bennion had advocated as early as the 1940s. Packer was a fierce believer in the power of unadulterated doctrine and worried about it getting watered down or compromised by secular philosophies: "True doctrine, understood, changes attitudes and behavior. The study of the doctrines of the gospel will improve behavior quicker than a study of behavior will improve behavior. Preoc-cupation with unworthy behavior can lead to unworthy behavior. That is why we stress so forcefully the study of the doctrines of the gospel" (Packer 1986). This was part of a larger attitude of suspicion toward the idiosyn-cratic and personal that flavored Packer's approach to religious instruction in domestic, church, and educational contexts alike. He was known to discourage those speaking in church worship and at funerals from using personal narratives and talking too much about experience and to instead focus on doctrine.

Packer clearly shared Bennion's concern with moral action, but he believed the catalyst of moral reformation was an offering of doctrine seemingly in isolation from direct experience. Bennion agreed that too much preoccupation with the self and with "right" behavior could become counterproductive, but, as we noted earlier, he was adamant that there was no such thing as an objective or innocent presentation of doctrine and that therefore it was best to be clear about the motivations and experiences that shaped interpretation. Indeed, to fail to have such motivations would be a lost opportunity: "No one, whether working in the arts, in philosophy or in religion, will contribute richly in his specialized field if he fails to keep in touch with the life common to all men and to live it fully" (Bennion 1959, 96). Doctrine brought into relation with academic disciplines and with lived experience humanized and contextualized belief within the particular setting of one's life and time and enabled its vitality.

Packer's compartmentalized view drew a strict distinction between secular and sacred knowledge that has remained influential in the LDS Church's approach to religious education. Although this view intended to protect LDS teachings from the influence of secular ideas, it also risked narrowing their reach. Bennion feared that a religious identity formed around such an understanding of doctrine would forge a defensive identity against "the world" and worldly learning and become so brittle that, when confronted with contradiction, it could shatter. If the gospel couldn't point the way to a life of meaning in the very particular circumstances of one's life, it would become unattractive and unusable. Today, the LDS Church Educational System—with its various universities and institutes and seminaries—still stands uniquely poised to offer the integration Bennion advocated and to promote a more rational faith. Latter-day Saints, however, continue to struggle for more robust theological understandings of what academic disciplines might mean in the life of a Christian disciple, and part of the reason is the "regularized crisis" that O'Dea observed: many LDS educators today worry that, if they were to attempt to offer the kind of robust integration the LDS Church says that it wants, the effort might not be welcome.

For most of its history, the Church of Jesus Christ of Latter-day Saints has managed to maintain, with unusual success, its continuity from its almost

Dionysian explosion of prophetic vision and teachings in the nineteenth century to its more Apollonian curation of an emergent priestly tradition since. Part of what has helped that success is the insistence of its highest leaders throughout church history that they are not infallible and that every member has the responsibility to be educated, to act according to conscience and agency, and to seek their own personal witness of divine truths. But, of course, despite such teachings, currents in Latter-day Saint church life remain that squelch conscience and shame those who wish to offer criticism of church life or who debate teachings of church leaders. And the LDS Church still wrestles with the paradox of believing itself to be led by prophetic revelation that is also, at the same time, continual and therefore subject to further revision or change. Church leaders have articulated and defended the special authority of apostolic witnesses who stand at the head but have said less about the dangers of excessive or categorical trust or about what faithful criticism might look like. Neither are there clear institutional practices of renouncing and taking responsibility for errors of the past.[5] This was, Bennion felt, a role he and others could and should play, as long as they offered their critiques in the interest of honoring the higher good his church always aimed for. His own rational faith made him a critic, but what he liked to call a "loving critic," someone who was invested in assisting the institution in its high ambition to enable universal human self-realization.[6] The terms on which such criticism would be welcomed today remain unclear.

A certain kind of embarrassment has persisted in LDS culture about that part of religion that Bennion insisted was "of man" and that is, ironically, the very reason for the need for the continual revelation that LDS theology champions. Recent developments suggest a willingness to take a wiser course. Church curricula are now more widely influenced by recent Gospel Topics essays that cover a variety of controversial topics in church history and doctrine, including a landmark essay, "Race and the Priesthood," which largely follows the logic of Bennion's thinking.[7] Although he never directly stated so in print, he believed the priesthood ban had its origins in human prejudice and not in God (something the essay alluded to acknowledges as a possibility) and that only through the process of testing the ban against reason, against the wisdom of scripture, and against the highest principles of the gospel, as he had advocated, would higher understanding and further revelation become possible. In other words, Bennion felt it was obvious that until and unless church leaders and members alike could admit the possibility of their own prejudice and see the contradictions of the policy, God would not be able to communicate His will to lift the ban.

Bennion labored to protect the LDS Church but mainly from itself. As an educator who was keen on opening minds to the wonders of the academic disciplines and who believed that Mormonism was "humanism in a religious context," he was less worried about the dangers of secular ideas and more worried about the misuses of religion that stem from willed ignorance and a compartmentalized spirituality. The reason is that he saw protectiveness of the exceptional nature of revelation as an approach of fear that would not allow the conditions for full self-realization in a religious context. He believed in a rational faith that would instead boldly and confidently and endlessly seek higher understanding through the work of humble self-reflection, moral attunement, and greater study and deliberation.

This was the work of dialogue, a principle he held dear. He asserted that "I have confidence inspired by decades of public discourse that, if both of us will keep talking and keep listening, the results will please us both. It is impatience with another's point of view, an insistence on immediate action, the exercise of power before that process of dialogue occurs, or imposition of a policy without willingness to explain, listen, patiently explain again that I mistrust" (1988a, vi). There was no reason for Bennion to believe that impatience, incuriousness, control, or refusals to listen would be any less damaging to the ongoing human dialogue with God. When believers adhere as best as they can to the fundamental principles of doing justice, loving mercy, walking humbly before God—that is, when "religious belief [extends] outward," as we will next explore—they maximize the good and minimize the damage of the wrong thinking they might do in the name of faith (1988a, vi).

Social Morality

Lowell Bennion's most lasting legacy is undoubtedly his exceptional example of ethical action and, for our purposes here, his decades-long articulation and defense of social morality in the context of Latter-day Saint belief, a work to which no other Latter-day Saint scholars have dedicated themselves with such thoroughness before or since. In his personal and professional lives, Bennion was tireless in his dedication to service and relentless in his insistence that service of the most underprivileged was central to the education of young people and to Christian discipleship. In his writing and teaching, he wanted to draw down the power of religion to focus not on a world and life to come but, using spiritual hope as a catalyst, on the lived conditions of God's children on this earth and in this life. Toward the end of his life, he admitted that, after so many years of service, "I have less interest in salvation than I used to have. I don't want to be exalted. I'd like to be in the presence of Christ, but I believe that he who would save his life shall lose it, and he that would lose his life shall find it" (1985b, 17). In other words, it wasn't the idea of exaltation but aspiration to it that bothered him, especially when it got to the point that desire for exaltation replaced or was pitted against ethical concern for civic society. His sense of ethics was inspired by his father, by his own careful reading of the scriptures, and by the impact of like-minded theologians, most notably Albert Schweitzer (1875–1965), whom he read as a PhD student at the University of Strasbourg where Schweitzer had once attended.

Schweitzer began his professional career as, at once, a brilliant organist and musical scholar and a theologian. He had, however, long harbored a desire, as he describes in the autobiography that Bennion encountered shortly after its publication in 1933, to follow Jesus and lose himself in service of the neediest. This eventually led Schweitzer to obtain a medical degree, to commit to decades of service in Africa, and to articulate his philosophy of reverence for life, for which he would eventually win the Nobel Peace Prize in 1952. Schweitzer relished the experience of moving from the theoretical to the practical, and he saw this move not as a heroic gesture but as a natural extension of his love for life and learning. As he wrote,

> only a person who finds value in any kind of activity and who gives of himself with a full sense of service has the right to choose an exceptional task instead of following a common path. Only a person who feels his preference to be a matter of course, not something out of the ordinary, and who has no thought of heroism but only of a duty undertaken with sober enthusiasm, is capable of becoming the sort of spiritual pioneer the world needs. (Schweitzer 2014, 88)

It is perhaps easy nowadays to feel some suspicion of self-service in an autobiography that describes Schweitzer's own antiheroic heroism and that is framed by the colonialist paradigm of the white savior. Bennion does not seem to have felt such criticism of Schweitzer's autobiography, a book he returned to a handful of times in his life, helping to give shape to his own life as a spiritual pioneer. Indeed, he had clearly harbored similar desires. The antidote to the vainglories of the academy and religion's temptations to self-righteousness was community service, something to which he devoted himself with a similar "sober enthusiasm." He firmly believed, however, that to make service self-serving contradicts Christian virtue. So important was this to him that he significantly never wrote an autobiography, was not a fan of even keeping a journal, and gave reluctant permission for a biography shortly before he died. He garnered several awards toward the end of his life, including the Outstanding Citizen of the Decade by the Salt Lake County Commission in 1989, inclusion in the Hundred Most Caring People in America by the Caring Institution in DC in 1989 and in a book that featured the one hundred most caring people in history (which included Schweitzer) in 1992, and official recognition from the Utah state legislature and the governor for his lifetime of service in 1992. He repeatedly expressed discomfort, however, in receiving recognition for service that should be the norm of life. Even though his own step into service was gradual and less dramatic, his commitment to local service avoided the potential trappings of a colonialist model and pointed to a more mundane and actionable pattern for others. But it should not go unremarked that Bennion's theology of service, like Schweitzer's, assumes the subject position of the person of privilege (the "we" that should serve "them") and is not centered on the experience of the sufferer of injustice, as in the work of the African American theologian Howard Thurman, which would be so influential on Martin Luther King Jr. and the civil rights movement.[1]

Bennion's social morality was a commitment to the improvement of the social, spiritual, and economic conditions of the disadvantaged to unleash their full potential, which, in his mind, was a natural extension of his Latter-day Saint values: "our task is to find effective ways of helping our minority brothers to help themselves. They cannot lift themselves up by their own bootstraps. We do not live in a land of equal opportunity for all because in today's world opportunity depends on resources, on health, money, education, and self-respect—which are not equally available in America or in the world" (England 1988, 252). The kingdom of God begins in the individual heart, where affections and values are chosen, but it also seeks to become a society that promotes the abundant life for all. As a consequence, it behooves the believer to work for both personal and social integrity.

His social morality is most developed in three books primarily: *The Book of Mormon: Guide to Christian Living* (1985a), *Do Justly and Love Mercy: Moral Issues for Mormons* (1988b), and his study of the Old Testament, *The Unknown Testament* (1988b). In the last-named book, he joins the Christian modernists in their belief that "the Old Testament affirms that there can be no true spirituality without genuine social morality. . . . This concept is called ethical monotheism, Judaism's finest contribution to the world, in my opinion. God is ethical. And those who would serve him must also be ethical in their human relations" (Bennion 1988b, 47). That responsibility, he insisted, must be characterized by "justice and compassion" as "the hallmarks of social mortality" (Bennion 1988a, 11).

As discussed earlier, Christian fundamentalism emerged in the early 1900s in reaction to Christian modernism and its emphasis on ethics, and many leaders of the LDS Church joined in that criticism, as we saw in the case of J. Reuben Clark. Many Christian conservatives believed that an emphasis on ethics stemmed from an embarrassment about the doctrinal claims of Christianity, and there was certainly some truth to the claim.

Fundamentalism, however, was also a reaction against the political climate of the time. The New Deal of President Franklin Delano Roosevelt during the 1930s was a very popular program among many Christians and no small number of Latter-day Saints but came under the criticism of some Christian leaders, including Heber J. Grant, then president of the LDS Church, for fear that it would discourage self-reliance. The growing concerns of subsequent LDS leaders about the evils of communism built on Grant's concerns and helped to establish a conservative ethos that would predominate in LDS culture for decades to come. Bennion had progressive political leanings, to be sure, but he did not so much see himself in opposition to conservative concerns as a loving critic of their excesses. Even though he was sympathetic to the arguments about ethics offered by Christian modernists, he was, in the end, uninterested in polemics and instead worked to avoid the rhetoric and trappings of contemporary debates and focused his arguments on scriptural interpretation and sound reasoning. His ability to offer insights that were responsive but not beholden to contemporary discourse was a hallmark of his moral and intellectual genius. It is only surprising that his gentle and inviting spirit and the careful scriptural and nonideological rhetoric he employed didn't find more traction in the LDS ethos.

Social Morality

For Bennion, the grounds for social morality were simple: if every individual has inherent worth and divine potential, as LDS theology postulates, and a fundamental need to discover and creatively express his or her purpose, then society—homes, churches, schools, and governments—should be organized to the end of enabling the discovery and pursuit of that purpose. "God is an ethical being," he explains, "a person of integrity and compassion, deeply committed to the well-being of his children, who have been created in his image and likeness. Because we are in the divine image, we too must be just and merciful" (*Bennion* 1988b, 152). He went as far as to claim that such an understanding would be the solution to world peace: "Until we learn to hold human life—every human life—sacred, we shall not have peace on earth" (152). As should be evident in the way he prioritized his loyalties, he worried about any beliefs that lost sight of the centrality of human worth and human society: "Theology is of no value if it substitutes for social morality. Devils also believe and tremble. To be righteous, belief must include concern for our fellow human beings. Religious ordinances and rituals are vain if they do not encourage spirituality and morality. Church life is not an end in itself but a place to be inspired to go forth and deal honestly and compassionately with each other" (Bennion 1988b, 47–48). It was the outward thrust of one's moral concern that represented for Bennion the ultimate test and fruition of Christian faith. "The heart of Christian discipleship," Bennion states simply, "is service" (1985a, 81).

Schweitzer had articulated something very similar: "By his spiritual nature [Christ] was in fact the ethical master promised by the prophets" (Schweitzer 2014, 109). Perhaps no one in American Christianity had expressed such ideas with more force than Walter Rauschenbusch in his formidable *Christianity and the Social Crisis* of 1908. In it, he wrote,

> No man is a follower of Jesus in the full sense who has not through him entered into the same life with God. But on the other hand no man shares his life with God whose religion does not flow out, naturally and without effort, into all relations of his life and reconstructs everything that it touches. Whoever uncouples the religious and the social life has not understood Jesus. Whoever sets any bounds for the reconstructive power of the religious life over the social relations and institutions of men, to that extent denies the faith of the Master. (2008, 42)[2]

Bennion refused any such uncoupling and was convinced that the necessary freedom and opportunity for self-realization could not exist equally for all without vigilant, collective, and ethical service. Such service included acts intended to relieve suffering, as well as efforts to design and create opportunities in the civic sphere that might facilitate human flourishing. In a word, service should be at the very heart of a religious education. As he wrote,

> Every Latter-day Saint should serve his community as well as his church. . . . If we are to help solve the problems of mankind, we must prepare ourselves both spiritually through prayer and gospel study and also intellectually by reading and studying out of the best books. The problems we face are exceedingly complex, requiring *not only the ideals of the gospel, but also a realistic knowledge of economic, political, legal, and behavioral principles.* The world needs desperately . . . professionals who combine pragmatic knowledge with Christian idealism. (England 1988, 266–67, emphasis added)

Of course, one of the great questions of his age was the degree to which government regulations or programs are necessary or effective to achieve social ends. Like his more politically conservative fellow Latter-day Saints, he was profoundly committed to the inviolability of agency, but he believed it would be safeguarded not merely by a kind of vigilant protectionism that sought to identify threats but by methods, including the indispensable actions and programs of institutions, that could facilitate and encourage the creative use of agency. Individual agency, in other words, was not fully expressed by the absence of its opposition but by deliberate social encouragement. He believed that social and systemic obstacles to full self-realization were real and harmful and that "the government itself [need not] meet all of [one's] needs, but it should actively foster conditions favorable to satisfying . . . basic human needs" (1988a, 79).

Although the seeds were sown earlier in the twentieth century, political polarization began to increase in the 1970s and accelerated through the last two decades of Bennion's life. An interfaith coalition of conservatives that included Latter-day Saints began to gain momentum to claim conservatism as their rightful political terrain. Their causes were abortion, family, and the equal rights amendment, while an increasingly secular left gravitated toward civil rights, feminism, and the environment. The two major political parties, once overlapping in the political center, polarized and sorted themselves more and more according to region, class, race, and religion than ever before. The net effect was a growing alignment of a US Latter-day Saint identity with the Republican party, making it harder for Bennion's ideas, grounded though they were in careful readings of scripture, to gain traction except among the already and increasingly fewer progressive-minded Latter-day Saints. This is a special shame because Bennion's emphasis on humanitarian service, which he taught and practiced long before the polarization started, could have provided an antidote to the trend toward polarization and led to greater political balance today among church members. He had long believed that service not only benefited others but also called forth and trained the creative use of agency beyond the self, focused attention on practical solutions, and moderated the extremes.

He certainly was more willing to roll up his sleeves in practice and to avoid the realm of theory and rhetoric than most conservatives and liberals, thus pointing the way to a more pragmatic social morality. Although he promoted liberal ideals and values, most notably in his chapter "Being a

'Liberal'" in *Do Justly and Love Mercy*, he was mainly interested in rescuing core principles and values of Christian living that he felt were also being sorted by political affiliation and lost in the political fray. As he put it,

> In reality, of course, there is no such thing as a liberal or conservative. Identifying reality with a term is a thinking phenomenon called reification, common enough but still an artificial limitation on the nature of reality. People are persons, not abstractions. Terms illuminate people but are not synonymous with them. We are sometimes liberal in the morning and conservative in the evening. Some are liberal about their own behavior and conservative about their children's. (Bennion 1988a, 85)

Commitment to service teaches what few armchair political pundits ever understand—that good government is hard work, that there is no silver bullet and therefore no clear and consistent delineation between good and evil parties. In other words, his was not an ideological but a pragmatic argument about social morality; he was a believer in the power of social reality to reveal the contours of which local actions should define a Christian call to service. While Latter-day Saints might not be able to agree in political philosophy, he hoped that they can be united in a commitment "to do justly and love mercy" and "to promote basic human rights in whatever economic and political order they live" (Bennion 1988a, 29).

Bennion argued against the partisan logic that forced a choice between the value of self-reliance and the value of compassion for those whose circumstances limited their freedoms: "I believe in taking full responsibility for my own feelings, thoughts, and actions and getting others to do likewise. But I also believe in recognizing that people are not always solely responsible for what they are and do. They have been shaped for good or ill by forces beyond their knowledge and in certain instances beyond their control" (1985a, 117). That knowledge was hard-earned by virtue of the thousands of relationships he had formed with individuals who suffered from social isolation and lived below their potential for uncountable reasons, many of whom were also compromised in their ability to treat themselves or others well. In an age where it is common to speak of the underprivileged in purely theoretical terms, it is important to remember that he never did so in the abstract. He was talking about friends.

Despite its belief in perfectibility, Latter-day Saint theology, he liked to point out, offered a compassionate view of human weakness. Christ suffered, according to Latter-day Saint scripture, not for sin alone but for "pains," "afflictions," and "sicknesses"—that is, the biological, social, and environmental conditions of life that inhibit one's ability to live up to one's potential. Alleviating suffering, for Bennion, was a way of participating in God's grace and atoning power of healing. Although he didn't oppose the idea of government programs as a solution to human suffering, he shared the conservative concern that bureaucracies are often ill-suited to addressing individual needs. This ethic was strongly articulated by Schweitzer and remained important to various iterations of personalism. Schweitzer had written, "One can save one's human life, along with one's professional existence, if one seizes every opportunity, however unassuming, to act humanly toward those who need another human being. . . . Everyone in his own environment must strive to practice true humanity toward others. The future of the world depends on it" (Schweitzer 2014, 90–91). Indeed, it wasn't the fear of creating dependency that worried Schweitzer and Bennion as much as the tendency of programs, even the best intentioned or religious ones, to ignore the dignity of the individual or even to humiliate the person in pursuit of institutional objectives.

Service, in other words, should not be offered on behalf of an ideal but on behalf of an individual person. It should not merely strengthen but widen one's social circle. The self-realization of every Christian requires a commitment to clearing the path of self-realization for all. This call for sociality and promiscuous friendship was the Christian opportunity for the abundant life: "All of us have the power to forge creative relationships. All we need is sincerity and interest in the welfare of others. People need assurance of our respect and acceptance, our interest in what they are doing, and our awareness of their worth as individuals. . . . And no one can have too many friends" (Bennion 1996, 107). He saw the importance of human relationships in simple, Christian terms: "My impression is that he [Jesus] spent more time discussing human relations than he did relations to God" (Bennion 1988a, 5). One should be as deliberate about friendship as about service: "True religion is more than piety, more than ritual, more than personal morality. These must be accompanied by social morality—by compassion and by wisely giving self and substance to others. True religion—say both Hebrew and the Book of Mormon prophets—is inseparable from high moral relationships with fellowmen" (Bennion 1985a, 120). If one commits to a collaborative spirit of friendship in the civic sphere, one finds the highest level of self-fulfillment "by co-operating with his fellow man in a 'free' society" and thus one "can increase the strength and effectiveness of [one's] own agency" (Bennion 1985a, 51). Being more aware and more responsible for the problems of society, in other words, has the added advantage of liberating rather than restricting one's own freedom, a conservative value.

Bennion did not believe that the call to relieve suffering was incompatible with the importance of accepting and preaching self-reliance. Social structures can and do exist that harm individuals, but individuals, especially those in positions of privilege, can dismantle such structures or build alternatives for the benefit of others. What this did require of all believers was a spirit of humility and respect for difference: "May those who profess discipleship of Jesus Christ cooperate in building his kingdom and—in the process—be willing to hear one another and then to respect or even reconcile their differences" (Bennion 1988a, 94).

What emerges from Bennion's thought is a sense of the human self that is both individual and unique but also deeply intersubjective and interdependent. While he always encouraged individual responsibility, "there are other times when it is well to remember the grace of God and Christ and [the efforts] of so many fellow human beings who have gone before us and of others still living" (Bennion 1983, 26). Grace, in other words, is not merely a divine but also a social gift to both receive and reciprocate. This legacy of inherited conditions is not a reason to conclude that agency is an illusion or that choices don't matter. Precisely because collective choices by others shape one's life so profoundly, each person is a steward of one's impact across society and across generations. Agency becomes, in Bennion's philosophy, more powerful than what a narrowly individualistic conception contemplates, but, for that reason, individuals must be taught to appreciate and use their role in shaping the larger social whole. He reminded his readers that "Latter-day Saints place a heavy emphasis on individual responsibility, growth, and salvation—on the righteous use of inalienable free agency. We also have an inspiring history of our efforts to create a Christian society. There is a great need to keep a balance by strengthening both the individual and society through our religious efforts" (Bennion 1988b, 75).

And, of course, the contingencies that shape our lives are not merely social. Bennion broke those contingencies into three main categories: "I put myself at the mercy of three powerful forces—nature, people, God—forces that are largely out of my control" (Bennion 1996, 21). This has significant implications:

> We "live, and move, and have our being" in each other as well as in nature and in the providence of Deity (Acts 17:28). We are enormously blessed by the contributions of our fellow human beings, by our social heritage. The comforts of life, freedom from many diseases, beautiful music, government by law, and the wisdom of ages past have come to us freely. On the other hand, we also suffer from acts of terrorism, drunken drivers, murder, rape, robbery, dishonesty, and deceit. We live uneasily under the threat of nuclear war, domestic violence, and a flood of illegal drugs. (Bennion 1996, 82)

In his study of the Book of Mormon, Bennion warned that a failure to acknowledge these three contingencies was a kind of selfishness that foolishly or naively "put ourselves in the center of life" (Bennion 1985a, 18). Fetishizing a narrow conception of individual human agency, in other words, can be a kind of controlling narcissism that demands that all of one's actions have identifiable and immediate corresponding consequences. This ironically risks rendering agency as a form of control over the agency of others and tends to judge the circumstances of one's and others' lives as just deserts. He insisted that Christianity didn't give human beings this right. Christianity did grant the right to expect that choice matters first and foremost to one's own integrity, growth, and fulfillment. Moral choices are not those that guarantee good outcomes but those that stem from a growing selflessness that creates chances for others to shape their own lives well.

Despite the opportunities American society affords many, he knew intimately that chances for self-realization were severely compromised, especially for racial minorities, women, the poor, and the disabled and mentally ill. Neither the doctrine of human equality and eternal worth in the eyes of God nor the postulate of a free market or of a free society should be confused with the very real and unequal conditions of life: "Human beings are not equal in their native intelligence, artistic potential, anticipated longevity, or opportunities in life, but they are equal in their basic need for food, warmth, love, self-respect, creative self-expression, and response from other human beings. They are equal in their need for self-fulfillment and salvation" (Bennion 1983, 61).

Bennion's sense of a broad social morality was, by the time he wrote his "little books" in the 1970s and 1980s, against the grain of common Latter-day Saint thinking. The 1960s represented a great groundswell of public dissatisfaction with the morality that had been inherited from the postwar generation. It was, at once, a call to a new and broader social morality and a great sexual revolution that seemed to celebrate individuality at the expense of the collective whole. In reaction to these latter developments that directly challenged the sexual mores of Latter-day Saint life, the LDS Church doubled down on its expectations of sexual behavior. Although it eventually issued a statement generally in favor of civil rights, individual church leaders often criticized the movement as socialist in orientation and threatening to religion, despite the movement's notable religious roots. Today, the word *morality* in LDS culture today connotes mainly sexual mores, and individual honesty and character and its social dimensions are often neglected.

The consolidation of LDS conservative political leanings in the wake of the 1960s also made it more difficult for Bennion's concerns to find traction. He wanted laserlike focus on the disadvantaged at a time when the concept of social justice was increasingly anathema to conservatives. "On judgment day," he wrote, "Jesus will identify with the alienated of our society" (Bennion 1996, 34). To identify such people, Bennion took many of the ethical directives, particularly from the Old Testament, at their word. He explains, "Just as God is merciful, so he requires us to be merciful, particularly to those who have no particular claim on us: the poor, the widow, the stranger, the fatherless, and the afflicted (Bennion 1988b, 57). The poor, widows, strangers, and the afflicted were for Bennion individuals, often single mothers and people of color, who had often suffered the results of social immorality, of policies and prejudices and neglect that placed them at a disadvantage. Their circumstances didn't mean that they couldn't or shouldn't pursue a path of self-reliance. But it did mean that the privileged classes of society had a responsibility to establish greater equity. He saw families breaking apart and individuals falling into wayward paths in lives of suffering and despair. His sociological Mormonism allowed him to decry divorce, especially when it was the result of selfishness, but also to decry discrimination and poverty, knowing the strains that they could put on family relationships. He decried drug abuse and crime, but he also saw mass incarceration and the risks of recidivism as threats to family happiness. He insisted that members learn peace in their hearts and in their marriages, but he worried about the destructive power of war on all social structures. In other words, he consistently applied the same principles to the individual and to the collective society, insisting that morality was both individual and collective. He saw the relevance of Old Testament ethics all around him: "In contemporary life, [the teachings of Old Testament prophets] mean that we can spend less for armaments and more for health care, shelter for the homeless, food for the hungry, education, arts, and research. Who would not pray the Lord to hasten the day of fulfillment?" (Bennion 1988b, 146).

In his reading of the Old Testament prophets, religious worship and practice are morally acceptable only if they are committed to redressing inequalities and maximizing opportunities for self-realization for others. Perhaps the scripture he most frequently cited was from the book of Micah:

> Wherewith shall I come before the Lord, and bow myself before the high God? Shall I come before him with burnt offerings, with calves of a year old? Will the Lord be pleased with thousands of rams, or with ten thousands of rivers of oil? shall I give my firstborn for my transgression, the fruit of my body for the sin of my soul? He hath shewed thee, O man, what is good; and what doth the Lord require of thee, but *to do justly, and to love mercy, and to walk humbly with thy God?* (Micah 6:6–8 [KJV], emphasis added)[3]

As he once rephrased it for a contemporary audience, "The Lord would not have a people who were dishonest or unjust and who, while living in comfort, ignored the needs of widows and orphans" (Bennion 1996, 30).

Failure to understand and accept such social responsibilities stemmed from a failure to understand the whole and broad cloth of religion. Without social morality, a kind of moral schizophrenia could emerge in which religious communities take compassionate care of their own while remaining indifferent to or even judgmental about the suffering in the broader society. In the 1970s, Bennion acknowledged that his own racism as a young man arose because "the Gospel must have been fragmented if not pulverized. I must not have seen it in one piece, in a framework of fundamental concepts, as I am beginning to now. Nor was I particularly interested in the implications of the Gospel for the social issues of the day. High walls separated religion from daily life except in some areas" (England 1988, 249). To the degree that Mormonism retreated from the broader social sphere of responsibility and built those high walls, its legacy of a collective ethos became directed increasingly at the specific character of church life, dedicated mainly to the observances of religious practice and programs and to a sense of belonging and Latter-day Saint identity but less intensely focused on the extramural world. About the range and intensity of church programs, Bennion wrote, "We have a very elaborate program, so the faithful Latter-day Saint is pretty well preoccupied with church life, church activity, and tends to identify the religious life with church life. But that doesn't leave much time or motivation to go beyond the boundaries of the Church program into the larger community. That concerns me. . . . We should practice Christianity, not just Churchianity" (1985b, 14).

For this reason, Bennion brought an estimated thirty thousand Latter-day Saint students at the University of Utah over many years directly into contact with the poor, with widows, and with the sick in Salt Lake City and provided the experience of service.[4] He simply wanted to ensure that the LDS sense of morality was expansive enough to address the pressing concerns of his age:

> In addition to our families and Church members, there are other human beings who need our help. Alma points the way, tells us to treat all alike whether in or out of the Church. These people need visits, conversation, lawns cut, snow removed, houses cleaned, and yards cleaned. Physically or mentally handicapped individuals need comparable attention. One-half to two-thirds of the earth's population goes to bed malnourished while many of us fight the battle of the bulge. (Bennion 1985a, 122)

In perhaps his most succinct paraphrase of Old Testament ethics in contemporary language, he concludes that

> Beyond our baptism, confirmation, ordinations, prayers, and offerings to the Lord, he requires our mercy, compassion, love, and generosity to one another. We learn mercy by practicing the works of mercy. This means that we visit the widows and others who are lonely, succor the disabled of mind and body, provide work for the unemployed, take an interest in children who need attention, and help people become more self-sufficient both at home and abroad. It means that we are troubled by the suffering of fellow human beings and do something to relieve it. It also means that our sharing is somewhat selfless in that we do not praise ourselves for these works or criticize others for needing our mercy.

Nothing sours the sweetness of a loving act so quickly as the merest taint of self-congratulation on our generosity or sensitivity or tact!" (Bennion 1988b, 59)

It seems implied here, and is perhaps redundant to note, that what also sours the sweetness of a loving act is the merest taint of blame cast on the recipient who somehow should have known better and who better not come knocking for help again. Christian duty required a firm commitment in the life of every Latter-day Saint to feel and express compassion toward the most vulnerable without judgment: "We must set aside time, energy, and means to help low-income and lonely people, the elderly, the disabled, and the alienated—all marginal members of our community, whether they be members of the Church or not" (1988b, 59).

His social morality relied on Max Weber's distinction between the priestly and prophetic roles played by various Old Testament prophets. Weber's priests were those who primarily dedicated themselves to preserving the institution and securing the coherence of tradition while prophets were those who sought the liberation of the oppressed by calling institutions and people to repentance for ethnocentrism and pride. Bennion saw the value of the priestly class and the need for institutional consolidation and coherence, but Weber had helped him to see that, if left unchecked, the administrative impulse of organizational life and its associated rituals would suppress if not supplant the important prophetic work of distributing justice and mercy. Perhaps from the influence of the modernists and Schweitzer, Bennion drew inspiration from Old Testament prophetic voices, from the ethical monotheism of Amos through Malachi, that inspired believers to attend to the immediate social conditions of their society and to act scrupulously to alleviate suffering. Studies of ethical monotheism had suggested that Jesus signaled a transition to principles rather than rules but as the apotheosis, not a reversal, of Old Testament ethics. Bennion hoped that an ethical Mormonism could balance the ethical and practical orientation of the Mosaic law with the spirit of Christian principles:

The strength of the Christian ethic taught by Jesus lies in its positive emphasis on principle, leaving to us the method of applying the principle in our daily walk. Often, the high-sounding principle satisfies us and, because we do not actively do evil, we fail to practice our Christian love in concrete ways. The finer ethical-religious life, I believe, would be to combine the strengths of both the Judaic and the Christian ethics, being guided by the principle and taking specific, positive ethical action in the marketplace, in the community, in the family, and among nations. (Bennion 1988b, 90)

Bennion's was perhaps a uniquely Latter-day Saint approach to the question of the relationship between the two biblical testaments, since the Book of Mormon introduced Christian spirituality into the context of the Mosaic law and pointed to an ethical postmosaic Christianity. In his memorable summary of ethical Mormonism, *Do Justly and Love Mercy*, he concluded, "Faith, not morality, is religion's more distinctive gift; but in the teachings of the Hebrew prophets and of Jesus himself, morality had primacy. Religious worship and belief which ignored or contradicted justice and mercy were condemned" (1988a, 92).

The Marketplace and Materialism

An ethical Mormonism required some specifics, some attention to actual economic circumstances and choices that believers faced. Bennion's willingness to offer specifics stands alone among Latter-day Saint thinkers in the twentieth century, with the possible exception of Hugh Nibley, even though he joined a proud tradition that extends back to Brigham Young's prophetic leadership. Bennion worried that limiting a sense of responsibility to one's own person, family, and church community would give license to a spirit of unbounded business speculation and accumulation that Weber had seen in Protestant embrace of the rise of modern capitalism. Perhaps Bennion's ideas were too specific for his audience.[5] Young was not afraid to be specific. As he oversaw the economic foundations of a new civilization just beyond the contemporary boundaries of the US nation starting in 1847, Young served as a firebrand, both priest and prophet, who micromanaged the social morality of the Saints, often calling members to repentance for such things as overgrazing, wasteful consumption, giving in to the seductions of luxury, and failing to act on behalf of the collective good of others. As a champion of the collective ethos, he feared the infiltration of modern capitalism and the egocentric self-interest it inspired among Latter-day Saints.[6] An unfortunate and perhaps paradoxical byproduct of Young's protective outlook and fierce criticism of the consumerism of American life was the segregation of the Latter-day Saint community and identity and a concomitant tendency toward xenophobia and tribalism.

Bennion similarly wanted a social morality that embraced the responsibilities to the larger society while maintaining what he called religion's "renunciative tradition" of prophetic warnings, which he saw alive and well in both the Bible and in the Book of Mormon (1985a, 26). Unlike Young, however, Bennion made his peace with capitalism. He saw that the free market had many benefits, even though he also saw its excesses and believed it needed regulation guided by a strong moral culture of restraint. He did not, however, share the convictions of the harshest critics of socialism in America and in the LDS Church in the middle of the twentieth century who had little regard for the early Latter-day Saint collectivist pioneer efforts. He openly praised certain aspects of socialism, but because he was unflinching in his commitments to freedom of conscience and democracy, he ultimately preferred a well-regulated free market: "I fully subscribe to the necessity of child labor laws, safety laws for labor workers, anti-trust laws against monopolies, industrial insurance, federal bank insurance, and social security" (1988a, 27). In addition to regulations, the marketplace needed to be guided by the moral conscience of sellers and buyers alike; the behavior and moral neutrality of the marketplace should not be sanctified, in his word, with any kind of "halo" (1988a, 26). In this sense, he was a precursor to the moral critiques of the free market offered by such thinkers as Wendell Berry (2010) and more recently Jeffrey Sachs (2006).

He foresaw the dangers of marrying political ideology and economic philosophies with religion, because of the ease with which such marriages place the ideological cart before the theological horse. Instead of giving all their attention to the evils of socialism or the virtues of capitalism, the church and its members would be better served by exercising "judicious aloofness" when it came to political and economic ideologies (1988a, 25). Passionate belief in the righteousness of one party over another only signaled, in his mind, an elevation of partisan loyalty over theology, a subsequent impoverishment and narrowing of religious morality, and an empowerment of the somewhat arbitrary and capricious nature of political conviction. As his own life was winding down, he saw that decades of church leaders' anticommunist and antisocialist teachings were leading to a triumphant Republican claim on the Latter-day Saint political mind, consistent with the political sorting that characterized the United States in the 1980s and 1990s.[7]

Evidence shows that this sorting results when religion and politics become battlegrounds not over ideas or values but over a tribalized identity. Such sorting only reinforces those identities as people in the United States are increasingly unlikely to befriend someone across the aisle and unlikely to question the morality of their own political convictions.[8] Such alignments of identity in a culture that increasingly politicizes identity produce what Bennion feared: neglect of the principles and values that define morality for the Old Testament prophets and for Jesus and that otherwise motivate believers to serve in unfamiliar and marginalized spaces.

Bennion's conception of social morality was not intended to be a Democratic rejoinder against a perceived Republican theology. He sought a nonpartisan and ecumenical approach, antithetical to beliefs about one right party or even one right economic system for all nations and all circumstances. The detachment from party-driven morality he advocated requires of a religious person a kind of double-mindedness, an awareness that politics matter enough to require an unshakable commitment to civic engagement and the pursuit of good policy, but an awareness too that religious values expose the inadequacy of policy and the need for plurality and patience with the political process. Although the Church of Jesus Christ of Latter-day Saints continues to assert its political neutrality, especially as it has grown internationally, US Latter-day Saints remain among the most reliable Republican voters in the country. We might conclude, then, that it is not social morality but its absence that has contributed to an unhealthy marriage of theology and ideology for many Latter-day Saints. Indeed, a less socially engaged ethos for an international church might make it easier to define the cross-cultural and politically neutral terms of a Latter-day Saint lifestyle, but it would risk emptying that lifestyle of deep moral and social meaning and make it vulnerable to the trappings of ideological norms, rather than guided by religious principles and values.

Moralizing about the economy should not be confused with regulating it, although the latter certainly can follow from the former, something Bennion believed could be a positive outcome. A truly free market will not judge between a seller of vegetables and a seller of drugs, or between a casino and a hospital, and so he felt that some ethical specificity was needed:

> Today we live in a materialistic, pleasure-seeking culture. We build homes more spacious than our needs and furnished according to our fantasies.

Our closets are full of designer clothes and fashionable fabrics. We accumulate campers, boats, snowmobiles, VCRs, video cameras, motorcycles and other elaborate toys. We stretch ourselves at ease before the television, enjoying its sharp images and bright colors, and feel rewarded for our hard work. Moreover, we go to church on Sunday, say our daily prayers, give charity to good causes, and perhaps even keep a missionary in the field. I sometimes feel very uncomfortable about my own abundance. . . . [T]he God of Amos, Jesus, Alma and Mormon will not hear my prayers or take note of my worship if service is only an occasional interlude between seasons of working hard to add field to field, stock to stock, or gadget to gadget. (Bennion 1988a, 13–14)[9]

As we saw in the previous chapter, he insisted that a simpler life is more abundant because it allows the soul to expand and the thirst for distractions or possessions to decrease. He stated clearly, "The solution to materialism is simplicity" (1988a, 15). A simpler life was to him also more socially moral. Although he was not clear on how the negative impacts of excessive consumption could be measured concretely in the lives of others or in its effects on the environment, he understood that possessions shield us "from the distress of others" and make us less "people-minded" (1988a, 16, 17). Luxury was a sign of moral failure: "we are unchristian and inhumane to live in luxury in a world where so many lack adequate food, clothing, and shelter, let alone medical attention and education" (1988a, 44).

He found one of the most potent critiques of materialism in these verses from the Book of Mormon:

For behold, ye do love money, and your substance, and your fine apparel, and the adorning of your churches, more than ye love the poor and the needy, the sick and the afflicted. . . . Why do ye adorn yourselves with that which hath no life, and yet suffer the hungry, and the needy, and the naked, and then sick and the afflicted to pass by you, and notice them not? (Mormon 8:36–39)

About these verses, Bennion said simply, "It seems obvious to me that our culture must stand condemned before Moroni's accusation" (1985a, 25).[10] The Book of Mormon, in essence, was a defense of what he called the "nonmaterial values" of life such as humility, grace, integrity, honesty, and love, and a declaration that commitment to them inevitably meant concern for others.

Social Morality

In his contemplation of wealth from a Christian perspective, Bennion insists on the importance of integrity and honesty in how one earns wealth, concern for the well-being of others in how one uses it, and scrupulous attention to avoiding waste and luxury in why one wants it. He saw the dangers of an amoral marketplace that might allow someone to justify or at least condone business and consumption practices that, although legal, are morally harmful. Again, he was not unwilling to be specific. While it is obviously wrong to misrepresent what one seeks to sell, for example,

> It is equally wrong to tempt people to buy "junk" food, fad clothes, or other consumer goods with nothing to recommend them but current chic or a designer name by means of high-powered, misleading advertising. It is evil to make money by promoting alcoholic beverages, tobacco, other harmful drugs, prostitution, gambling, and like practices which destroy people's lives. To maintain integrity, a person should either be directly involved in producing meaningful goods or in supplying a service of real benefit to other human beings. (1988a, 43)

Other thinkers have perhaps avoided such moralizing because of the risks of oversimplification or even naïveté. For one, how can a business be held responsible for the immoral use of a product that is otherwise relatively benign? Even relatively healthy food can be overconsumed. What if the tax revenues from the sale of alcohol or even gambling were put to good use for education? Bennion didn't elaborate on these points, but he did call his readers to ask themselves, in the spirit of the Latter-day Saint concept of consecration, what is the good that God intends for me to do in this business venture, beyond my own self-interest in gaining wealth? He simply wanted a spirit of concern for others and a desire to bless society to become chief motivations behind all business practices and all economic activity. In essence, what should motivate the economy is the same thing that he argues should motivate government: "The protection of life, respect for free agency, and the promotion of social justice" (1988a, 77).

For Bennion, an ethics of the marketplace applies to producers and sellers as well as to buyers and consumers, and this is where his originality again breaks needed ground in the modern LDS context. He states, "I see a clear ethical imperative to stop wasting food, water, clothing, energy, and other natural resources" (1988a, 43). Modesty was to him an indispensable antidote to consumerism, which is not socialism but religious restraint: "We who have so much would do well to acquire one more thing—self-control" (1988a, 44). When the marketplace exercises too much influence, it results in the moral debasement of the human person, who is reduced to the role of a consumer. Avoiding this fate includes not just a proper management of money but an inventory of our values. Otherwise, we are driven to want and like things promoted by advertising: "we must evaluate our values and be sure they are truly ours, not just adopted wholesale from our environment" (1988a, 15). LDS ethics on questions of consumption have largely focused on the sexual and social mores implicit in entertainment but less on the inherent dangers of consumption of superficial, vacuous, or wasteful content. Bennion urges believers to take inventory on where they give attention and what they value: "we also need to scrutinize how we use our time" (1988a, 16). Filling our time with meaningful civic engagement is an especially potent antidote: "a meaningful way to practice social morality," he insisted, "is to join a worthy cause in the larger community" (1988a, 17). To be other-oriented in an economy that expects and incites self-focus and self-gratification is no small achievement.

The pursuit of luxury, by contrast, is all too easy. He did not suggest "that we should not have high-quality clothes, cars, houses, furniture. Quality is often less expensive in the long run. Luxury, however, by its very definition, means going beyond need. I also see a strong motivation of self-indulgence and vanity. It is childish to acquire something just because you can" (1988a, 45). To the degree that we have more than we need, in the spirit of the law of consecration, he reminded his readers of the "social uses of wealth" and the "great power" wealth affords to "bless others" (1988a, 45). He himself lived a modest lifestyle and never had as much money as he felt he needed because, as he noted, "I wish I had millions with which to provide work, housing, transportation, recreation, dental and medical care for the disabled, the poor, and underprivileged youth. I have concrete plans—plans which require money but which would help people in our society to help themselves" (1988a, 45).

Bennion wasn't critical of wealth per se, but he insisted on the moral principles that should guide our economic behavior. These were the fundamentals we discussed in the chapter 3: "The kingdom of God is within us, not in the cars we drive, the clothes we wear, or the houses we live in. The center of life is within us. How limited are external, material things in their capacity to satisfy the inner person! What one needs to satisfy one's soul is more integrity, freedom, creativity, and love—the finest attributes of God and humankind" (1988a, 47). Indeed, to be critical of government programs for their perceived spiritual harms while living in luxury far above reasonable need would be an especially flagrant display of hypocrisy.

Racism

Part of the genius of Lowell Bennion was how strictly he attempted to adhere to his best understanding of scriptural wisdom and how careful he was to maintain a value-based approach to social problems. In today's climate of political tribalism and hyperpolarization, it might be hard to believe that he wasn't primarily an ideologue, but the logical and scriptural presentation of his arguments was not proof-texting but rather a coherent theology of principles that could be consistently applied. In race relations, he found more opportunity for apply scripture:

> Either we apply the Gospel to our relations with all men or we perish both spiritually and perhaps mortally. Respect, love, and mercy for our neighbors are laws of life and cannot be ignored with impunity. Latter-day Saints should be in the forefront of the battle for equal civil rights for all groups in society. Latter-day Saints should give freely of their time and means to help the disadvantaged in our society and in the world to gain sufficient food, clothing, shelter, medical care, and self-respect. . . . [All of our religious observances] are vain unless we remember to "do justly and love mercy." (England 1988, 252)

Ultimately, Bennion felt compelled to state his moral opposition to racism clearly and unequivocally: "Racism is incompatible with our theology. If we believe in the Fatherhood of God, the brotherhood and sisterhood of humankind is a logical deduction. . . . Discipleship of Jesus Christ is incongruent with racial prejudice" (1985a, 116–17). His opposition to racism was always couched in the values of gospel living and was never aimed personally at any racism he perceived in his Church or its leaders. Although clearly disturbed by the priesthood ban, for example, he didn't take direct aim at leaders but instead steadily helped to build the theological context in which the ban and racism itself could finally be seen as incompatible with gospel principles.[11] To his mind, Mormonism wasn't just incompatible with racism; it was antithetical to it. Mormonism was an apotheosis of the notion of human perfectibility, or divination, as it is known theologically, and thus it expected all humankind to find fulfillment and joy in self-realization both in this life and in the life to come.

His progressive views on racism were also informed by what at the time was a somewhat unconventional reading of the Book of Mormon. I say unconventional because it was in the 1980s when then President Ezra Taft Benson began to emphasize the need for every member to read the Book of Mormon regularly. Benson had long believed that, in addition to its vital messages about Jesus Christ, the Book of Mormon provides a platform for understanding the divine destiny of the United States, the dangers of socialism that he saw described in the book's condemnation of "secret combinations," and the sanctity of freedom.[12] Benson's reading is not, on its face, incompatible with the book's strong critiques of racial and class bias, but it was not until more recently that scholars and church leaders alike have celebrated the book for its condemnation of class and racial bias. Indeed, the book's racial message was ambiguous enough (including a description of a curse of dark skin placed on Lamanites) so that, for earlier readers keen on defending the priesthood ban and steeped in anticommunist and anti-civil-rights sentiments, the Book of Mormon seemed to uphold the idea of divinely imposed intergenerational racial segregation.

Moreover, at a time when Latter-day Saint apologetics was increasingly focused on defending the book's authenticity and historicity, the reading Bennion offered in 1985 was decidedly theological and ethical in its orientation, highlighting its value for everyday Christian living in relation to others, and its application to a contemporary US social context. While the Book of Mormon upheld freedom as a central principle of all good government, he saw it as profound articulation that "all are alike unto God" and that therefore we bear social responsibility for the inequalities and harm that "false traditions" create to classes and groups. He wrote,

> No one who understands and believes the Book of Mormon can practice racial discrimination or be racist in any sense of the word. This is so despite the built-in race conflict between the Nephites and the Lamanites, a conflict recorded by the Nephites who only occasionally contrasted themselves favorably face-to-face with their Lamanite brethren. Alma reminds his people that "they brought upon themselves the curse; and even so doth every man that is cursed bring upon himself his own condemnation" (Alma 3:19). Many of us adopted prejudices from

our social environment and have spent our days ridding ourselves from them the best we can, trying to adopt the Book of Mormon philosophy. (1985a, 116)

This is an astute and subtle reversal of logic that some Latter-day Saints had used to theologize what otherwise had sociological explanations. Social science had given him confidence that "there is a reason for all behavior" and that we should therefore avoid judgment of others' behavior and instead focus on obtaining an understanding of what motivates it (1985a, 117). His sociological reading of the Book of Mormon sought the historical and psychological reasons behind the hatred that exists between the Nephites and the Lamanites and to which neither side is immune. In his own experience of diverse peoples, he noted that "I am convinced there is a basic equality among the so-called races and cultures of humankind. Differences are usually due to educational and environmental factors. The Book of Mormon challenges us to set aside our prejudices and to consider all individuals precious, one as another, no matter what their condition might be" (1985a, 118).

Bennion's reading of the Book of Mormon amounts to an argument that fighting racism, even forms that today are referred to as systemic or unconscious racism, requires taking critical inventory of cultural legacies, both individual and shared. He saw in society and in the book that many forces in society—what Book of Mormon prophets called "traditions of the fathers"—act on individuals to create conformity with norms that are morally harmful. Many Christian conservatives today, including some Latter-day Saints, worry that antiracism today is antithetical to the concept of moral agency, but Bennion's formulation of the problem of racism suggests that if we deny the possibility that various collective traditions over time can be shaped to either limit or expand opportunities for racial minorities, it is a defense of freedom that oddly implies that we are not free vis-à-vis tradition at all.[13]

It is unfortunate that in today's environment a nuanced position such as Bennion's has not been able to find traction in Latter-day Saint culture. While the culture war continued to debate whether socioeconomic conditions determine human opportunity, Bennion had insisted that human agency was never determined but always potentially compromised and conditioned by those conditions. Those conditions, however, were also what we collectively chose them to be. In other words, individuals and collective society both always had an opportunity to choose to make a difference both for oneself and for others. Agency, that is, although never absolute, was expansive and further-reaching than liberals and conservatives typically assumed and therefore required more, not less, moral creativity. Bennion understood that individual choices have shared qualities and deleterious effects that saturate the social network and, when amalgamated over time, can either block or facilitate development for individuals or groups of people. If citizens accept responsibility for social structures and use imagination and service to steer them in new and more beneficial directions, they will be using their own agency to create more and better choices for others. Until and unless citizens accept responsibility for inherited prejudicial attitudes, practices, and habits and seek to imagine them otherwise, human agency is hampered in its ability to produce a different future. By contrast, a defense of absolute individual autonomy, ironically, holds us back from such hard work by instead accepting the status quo. Bennion's plaintive questions posed in 1983 appeal to agency and resonate still:

> How long will it be before we will look beyond skin and even beyond culture and see in every human being a child of God and a brother or sister with the same fears, hungers, longings, needs, and joys that each of us has? How long will it be before we learn that God is no respecter of persons, that he has no favorites, that all are alike and equally sacred before him? How long will it take us to learn that to be a chosen people means simply to have the responsibility of serving our fellowmen for God? How long before we learn that what God has given to us, we should use to bless our neighbors? (Bennion 1983, 61).

Institutional Implications

Racial division, economic disparity, and other forms of inequality were for Bennion profane threats to the sacred order of Christian fellowship. Not only did he therefore want church members to choose their values carefully and to have more integrity in their application of values, but he also believed that the institution of the church could more proactively critique's society's failures and promote Christianity's highest social values. He insisted that "the Church should stand apart from any economic order and be concerned with justice, freedom, love, and good will among citizens" (1988a, 25). He wanted a stance of moral independence that would allow the church to weigh in on moral issues of the day without being partisan:

> No existing or socio-economic order is ideal or consistent with the principles of the gospel of Jesus Christ. Moreover, no one system is good for all countries and all cultures—nor is one political party best. I strongly feel that it is folly for the Church to become identified with a particular political party or economic order. Let the Church stand apart from capitalism, socialism, communism, and the Republican and Democratic parties. Let Church members be free to judge these economic and political philosophies and actions in the light of their own understandings of gospel principles. Let the Church encourage its members and all people everywhere to "do justly and love mercy" and to promote basic human rights in whatever economic and political order they live. (Bennion 1988a, 29)

He clarified what following his suggestion would look like: "In my view, the Church should be concerned with poverty, unemployment, education, health care fraud, and corruption in business and public life" (1988a, 82). He explained that, "in the tradition of the prophets of Israel—Amos, Hosea, Micah, Isaiah, and Jeremiah—the Church ought to play the role of moral critic of other institutions in society—business, government, family relations. Since it should have no political axe to grind and since its objectives are ethical, religious, and universal, it is ideally suited for the critic's role" (1988a, 82).

In the years since Bennion's death, we can see a willingness by the Church of Jesus Christ of Latter-day Saints to offer such a voice more frequently. The LDS Church has elevated a concern about racism, called for political civility, and championed humane treatment of immigrants and concern for LGBT rights. Although a promising trend, it may prove insufficient in this age of political polarization that has overrun US moral discourse and infiltrated LDS culture in recent years. The LDS Church's expressions of moral concern are not frequent and don't consistently cover all the relevant issues of the day, and they certainly are not always met favorably by members. They have, however, at least sought to make clear that Latter-day Saints should be guided by moral principles derived from their faith and not from their political party.

While there are institutional risks in saying too much, there are risks in saying too little. Bennion understood taking a moral position as a constant balancing act, but he insisted on the benefits of a principled and consistent approach by the church: "While I think it is true that a stronger stance could be frustrating to some members and potential investigators, I also believe that a strong and active stance on issues of social justice would be appealing to many members of the Church who find inadequate institutional expression for their social ideals and would also attract interested nonmembers" (1988a, 83). The church's reticence, for example, to speak out on environmental problems such as climate change or on the realities of police brutality or homophobia has led many members to conclude that these problems are either not real or not serious. The two political parties are more than capable of taking up any space vacated by a strong moral institutional voice and of inspiring moral concern for more narrowly defined policies and political identities. The vacuum leads to a greater tendency for people to identify primarily with their political party and only secondarily with their church or, worse, to equate their party with their religion, which leads to further distortion of the moral foundations of Latter-day Saint belief. Political parties are motivated by the prospects of victory more than by the challenge of building character or community, and the result is that they offer not points of moral concern but rather a warpath of vague moral outrage and fierce political tribalism. Indeed, since Bennion's time, the moral ground US citizens have ceded to political parties to determine right and wrong has made it very difficult for the moral voice of the church to maintain its independence and for Latter-day Saints to articulate and accept a nonpartisan, values-based call to social morality.

We can see, then, a consistent thread of concern that runs through Bennion's thought about the inherent and divinely appointed dignity and eternal potential of the human person that should organize personal morality and all institutional missions and behavior, from schools and churches to businesses and governments. When planted firmly and centrally in the soils of religious faith, the pursuit of truth and the entire enterprise itself of education can motivate a passion for greater understanding not for its own sake but for the sake of greater capacity to uplift and ennoble human life, both individually and collectively. Thomas O'Dea was not far off the mark, then, when he noted that one way out of Mormonism's challenge of integrating itself uniquely and successfully in the modern secular world was what one unnamed LDS educator advocated: we should organize institutions and society around the ethical principles of the Old Testament prophets and the teachings of Jesus—magnified by Mormonism's exceptionally promising concept of humanity's divine potential—in order to protect and promote the dignity and flourishing of the human person (O'Dea 1957, 238). In so doing, religion can find its much-needed place in a world hungering for meaning and joy.

CHAPTER FOUR

Bibliographic Essay

While this book has provided an overview of the most significant ideas in Lowell Bennion's books, it would be helpful to have a brief survey of what I consider to be his finest works and some thoughts about their strengths that might inspire readers to seek out and make use of his books, which are little appreciated today. He published fifteen manuals for the church from 1934 to 1968 and, in 1972, he published three books with Deseret Book, two on marriage and one on being a college student. Beginning with the publication of *The Things That Matter Most* in 1978, he published another ten "little books," including a final selection of his writings, *How Can I Help?*, published posthumously in 1996. He also left an unpublished manuscript on *Selected Wisdom from World Religions*.

In addition to writing books, he regularly gave speeches and published dozens of essays in such venues as the *Millennial Star, Week-Day Religious Education, Improvement Era*, and then, no longer employed by the church or, it appears, wanted in official church venues, in the later years of his life in the independent journals *Dialogue* and *Sunstone*. His early years as the author of manuals and as a teacher shaped his accessible writing style and provided an important foundation from which he ventured into new iterations of his thinking. There is a remarkable consistency to his thought over the course of his long writing career and, as is common with long-time teachers, some repetition of stories, scriptural interpretations, and ideas. His writings focused on many topics, including the fundamental teachings and beliefs of the Church of Jesus Christ of Latter-day Saints; guidance for how to read the accepted scriptures of the church and a survey of their most important insights, including the Old and New Testaments and the Book of Mormon; the need for and the reach of social morality; the importance of equality and other principles of successful courtship and marriage; insights drawn from other religions; and the Christian principles of successful leadership and teaching.

Two books that appeared toward the end of his life provide exceptional clarity and power and the most comprehensive overview of the themes that preoccupied him during his career. The first, *The Best of Lowell Bennion: Selected Writings 1928–1988*, was assembled with Bennion's consent and published in 1988 by Deseret Book and was edited by Eugene England. The book includes some excerpts from his books and even from his missionary diary, but its most valuable contribution, in addition to its marvelous introduction by England, is the survey it provides of his most important essays, several of which are worth mentioning here. England includes, for example, Bennion's 1966 "For by Grace Are Ye Saved," an essay published in *Dialogue,* which was an early treatise on the doctrine of grace that had fallen, in his view, into neglect and that has in recent years received renewed attention. He brilliantly redefines works not as a way of earning but of receiving God's love: "what we do by our own effort is *to prepare ourselves to receive the gifts of Deity*" (England 1988, 116). He further insists that God's gifts are not earned but "born of love, of grace." The collection also includes a selection of his best writings on social morality, including "The Church and the Larger Society" from 1969, "What It Means to Be a Latter-day Saint" from 1959, and a remarkable previously unpublished essay from the early 1970s, "Overcoming Prejudice." In the first essay, he insists that the world cannot be escaped but must be met with courage, preparation, and love to meet the "basic need of every human being, regardless of race, creed, or nationality, to feel his worth, to enjoy the dignity of self-respect" (England 1988, 267).

In a section of essays on love and marriage, Bennion writes about relationships between the genders at greater length than I have had the space to explore in this book. Bennion spent years counseling and advising young single adults and young married couples, and this resulted in a variety of publications and speeches, including one General Conference talk, on the topic of courtship and marriage. Despite his consistent use of male-gendered language that was typical of his time, he was a fierce advocate of the need for an equality of opportunity for women and men in education and careers. Self-realization was vital to him. And he was astute in his definition of love as more than a feeling of affection: "Peace and happiness will come to the world when we learn to love our fellowmen and learn to express that love in a manner *that will be acceptable to them, consistent with their need for freedom, creativity, and self-respect*" (England 1988, 230, emphasis added).

How Can I Help? offers Bennion's final parting wisdom that he hoped would help people to live happier lives more dedicated to effective service of others. It is a marvelous summary of his wisdom gathered over a lifetime, echoing themes that had preoccupied him as early as the 1930s and had carried through his entire career. It focuses on the young and includes chapters about sex and dating, self-control, and facing adversity and concludes with a moving call to live a holistic, simple, creative, and selfless life. In its expansive vision, its integration of his many ideas, and its ready applicability, it may be his finest work. He also makes some of his boldest statements about gender equality, including this:

> [Women] have the same hunger to express themselves creatively. They have a right to self-realization that comes with learning and growing intellectually and socially. . . . If you are a young woman, consult your desires, ambitions, and needs. Do not accept any limitations that someone may try to place on you either directly or by innuendo, because they think a particular activity or goal is "not appropriate" for a young woman. (*How Can I Help?*, 1996, 49)

Do Justly and Love Mercy: Moral Issues for Mormons from 1988 contains Bennion's most ambitious description of social morality. I have already quoted somewhat extensively from the book, but I will add that the essays explore a range of social issues that he felt preoccupied Latter-day Saints at the time and were in need of better scriptural wisdom and reasoning to guide believers, including women's rights and sexuality, civil rights and racism, wealth, authority, and the sanctity of life. On the topic of women, he offered practical and needed suggestions for better inclusion of women in church life that have been recently echoed by Neylan McBaine's *Women at Church* (McBaine 2014). The topic of the sanctity of life was inspired by Albert Schweitzer's concept of "reverence for life," and Bennion's essay focuses on the issues of abortion, capital punishment, and war. Spoiler alert: he is opposed to all three, although his opposition to abortion is somewhat nuanced:

> It is wrong to take the life of a potential human being because it makes both individuals and society callous toward the sanctity of life itself. ... any social system or philosophy that cooperates with underlying human selfishness in allowing people to avoid the consequences of their actions erodes the individual integrity which lies at the foundation of all moral order. It is my regret that the consequences, in this case, fall with disproportionate weight upon the woman, rather than equally upon both the woman and the man; but this inequity does not shake my profound conviction that casual abortion is a serious wrong. (Bennion 1988a, 63)

Environmental stewardship never found its way into this chapter and only briefly and infrequently in his writings, even though it would have been consistent with his thinking and with LDS doctrine for him to have treated the topic more extensively. Although the book has a chapter on sexuality and offers a rigorous defense of the importance of sexuality and equality, it also does not address homosexuality, a topic Bennion avoided. A strong advocate for creative sexual expression in marriage, he also had a strong distaste for sexual licentiousness. Faced with the availability today of marriage for gay men and women, it is likely that he would have made peace with any path, especially in the civic sphere, that provided an integrated and balanced approach to sexuality and that refrained from any justifications of self-gratification. At the same time, despite being a confirmed liberal with a profoundly compassionate heart, he might have found himself averse to the identity politics of sexuality today and agreed with church leaders who have recently warned against the tendency to place such identities ahead of a divine inheritance as sons and daughters of God.

Many Latter-day Saints today who are grateful for Bennion's opposition to the ban on the priesthood for men of African descent see the LDS church's opposition to gay marriage in a similar light, as a violation of fundamental rights and a barricade to full inclusion. Bennion saw poor, insufficient, and often invented theological justifications for the priesthood ban that contradicted fundamental principles. I cannot conclude that he saw similar theological contradictions with homosexuality. If anything, the

Bibliographic Essay

LDS Church's official and long-standing theology of heteronormativity that pervades even its understanding of godhood stood in the way for him to be fully accepting of homosexuality on moral grounds. The predominant understanding of LDS theology during his lifetime, of course, assumed that homosexuality was a choice. We do not have evidence that he ever questioned that assumption, although it is certainly possible. At least initially, he seems to have struggled to understand homosexual desire as anything but a chosen perversion of heterosexual norms. He might have eventually concluded that such heteronormativity needed correction. He certainly saw the high price his own son had to pay for his sexuality, but heteronormativity was deeply embedded enough in revelation to have justified, for him, some patience. It is also clear, however, that his theology already allowed for the possibility that nature imposed certain conditions on individuals and that everyone should be given full opportunity for self-realization and that the particular gifts of individual lives should be welcomed fully into the bosom of social belonging. There is no doubt that he would be fully supportive of the greater openness we have seen in recent years toward homosexuality in the LDS Church and would have encouraged more efforts to identify and root out bigotry. One can imagine that he would be vigilant and ask pointed questions about poorly reasoned justifications for prejudice and bias and would have kept his focus on the need for policies and practices that will facilitate the flourishing of the whole person, no matter their sexual orientation.

I have quoted generously from *Religion and the Pursuit of Truth*. I believe it is an exceptionally fine book that offered a consistent and integrated vision of education within the context of LDS theology. I suspect it will feel somewhat dated to some readers, not because its principles are outdated but because the contemporary debates about the role of religion in education have changed so dramatically since then. The book, to my mind, offers a blueprint for a similar book that could successfully tackle the contested question of religion's role in higher education today. It is a shame that Latter-day Saint educators have not sought to write more books of this kind to guide students and to do the work of connecting LDS teachings to contemporary circumstances and to various academic discourses. As I have indicated, I lament the relative paucity of such writing in LDS culture. I believe his story stands as a reminder for the need of a sustained, trusting, and generous spirit of dialogue at church-owned universities that will inspire the courage and experimentation necessary to produce the best thought.

I have mentioned that his approach to the Book of Mormon is somewhat unique in that he departed from the persistent anxiety in Mormonism over the status of the Book of Mormon's historicity. Early on, he felt a desire to prove its historicity through anthropological and other means but nevertheless decided that its truthfulness lay in its theology. His emphasis, again, is on the moral force of scripture; its truthfulness is manifest in its ideals and the ready applicability of those ideal to lived experience. The book is, like his other "little books," brief, but it packs in a tremendous amount of insight, allowing Bennion to apply the exceptional wisdom of the book to a wide variety of topics relevant to contemporary readers, including spiritual and material values, withstanding temptation, service and leadership in the church, human equality, the principles and ordinances of the gospel, and self-rule and the goodness of God. I would argue that we didn't see the kind of moral and theological attention he gave to the Book of Mormon until the last decade, with the emergence of the Mormon Theology Seminar and the 2020 publications on the books of the Book of Mormon by the Maxwell Institute.

A book that I believe holds up exceptionally well is *I Believe* from 1983, a collection of short reflections on basic principles and doctrines that had come to have personal meaning to Bennion. He covers such fundamentals as his belief in Christ, grace, repentance, and forgiveness but also such creatively conceived subjects as "a positive acceptance of life," "increase, growth, improvement," and "harmony between social science and religion." It is closer to the personal and testimonial writing that has come to predominate much LDS devotional literature and American memoirs. I say that with some important qualifications. Bennion strenuously avoided the personal and he was almost always laconic and short on detail. And so, to the degree that he is personal in this book, it is still a far cry from a memoir or confessional book. That said, his normal modus operandi is to appeal to scripture, reason, and context and to use minimal footnotes and citations in order to persuade his reader. In this book, he simply adds a more personal touch to this approach. His rational and scriptural approach had its merits, not the least of which was that it helped him to avoid letting his life story and his personality become an unhealthy and unproductive focus for his admiring readers. He did all that he could to avoid the cult of personality that engulfs so many popular American and Latter-day Saint writers. But it also came at some cost, since it tended to produce books that, although written with clear and accessible prose, did not make his inner life accessible. Again, *I Believe* is not exactly a confessional book, but its first-person point of view gives it a ring of authenticity and honesty that is endearing and effective. It also provides a gentle corrective to a growing tendency he saw in LDS culture to fetishize "knowing" by spiritual means that which is true. His first-person emphasis on what he believes, rather than on what he knows, betrays a humble and dynamic sense of faith, even as it also places emphasis on the power of experience. It places Bennion on a journey that appeals to the reader for its adventurous qualities rather than at a destination to which he condescendingly invites us.

I conclude with these moving words from his introduction to *I Believe*, which I believe characterize the power of his lifelong invitation to dialogue. I note here the hint of nostalgia for a childlike faith that is blended with a mature rejoinder about the value of the sobering and tempering effects of life. His faith here is both sturdy and pliant; his religion is the scaffolding and structure that give his faith the quality of a journey and allow a dynamic process of growth and change that is nevertheless steady and directed toward the things that matter most:

> What follows . . . is not my last will and testament. It is how I think and feel about some things in my religion today. My religion is not fossilized; rather, it is more like a living tree—not brittle like a Chinese elm, its branches breaking in every wind and storm, but more like a sturdy oak with weeping willow branches grafted in.
>
> There are fleeing moments when I wish I had the faith of a child. I hope my faith has retained some elements of a childlike faith—curiosity, openness, readiness to forgive, some trust. But I am not a child, and I can no longer think and feel as one. I have read books and have experienced tragedy, failure, sin, remorse, and doubt as well as thinking, learning, joy, and ecstasy.
>
> Your life, like mine, is characterized by multiplicity and change. Religious beliefs provide an anchor that can give security, continuity, and direction to life. They provide aspiration, hope, purpose, and excitement to living. But religion will do these things only if it is a dynamic, growing experience relating fruitfully to the whole of our feeling, thinking, and living.

The following essays, I hope, will stimulate thought, arouse feeling, and move us to action. (Bennion 1983, 2–3)

If thinking matters because of what it might inspire us to do and become and is to be measured by its effectiveness to that end, there has never been a more moral and more effective educator in the Latter-day Saint tradition than Lowell Bennion.

Notes

Chapter One. The Life of a Mormon Educator

1. For a history of the speech and its influence on church education, see Scott Esplin's essay, "Charting the Course: President Clark's Charge to Religious Educators " (Esplin 2006).

2. Important reflections on the lives and friendship of the three men are found in Goldberg, Newell, and Newell (2018). See also Thomas Blakely's "The Swearing Elders" (Blakely 1986).

3. This theory was later taken a step further and arguably too far by one of Lowell's most vocal students, Eugene England, who insisted that the ban was a cross to be borne by white antiracists and was ultimately punishment for white prejudice (Givens 2021, 88).

4. Smith's reluctance to accept geological findings were symptomatic of a larger suspicion toward evolution as well, felt by many church leaders. As a result, the teaching of evolution would not begin officially and in earnest at church schools until the early 1970s, and, even then, teachers of evolution continued to face innuendo, controversy, or opposition.

5. For a more in-depth analysis of Christian modernism, see *The Modernist Impulse in American Protestantism* by Hutchison (1992).

Chapter Two. The Abundant Life

1. Buber's philosophy of the I–Thou relationship was influential on humanistic psychology, particularly in the work of Abraham Maslow and Carl Rogers. It was also an inspiration to the civil rights movement and its emphasis on reversing the deleterious effects of objectification.

2. My reader will note that Bennion frequently used the gendered term *man* in reference to humankind, as was common in his time. Throughout this study,

when I quote him, I have left the terminology as it is originally found in his writings. Even though he was limited by this terminology and was not always capable of seeing the existence and limitations of sexism, he was nevertheless a frequent voice for gender equality.

3. See, in particular, his book *An Early Resurrection* and his definition of sin in *Letters to a Young Mormon*.

4. Three such ranches are the Birch Creek Service Ranch in Spring City, Utah, and Quickwater and Sky Ranch camps in Victor, Idaho.

5. My collection of creative nonfiction essays in *Learning to Like Life: A Tribute to Lowell Bennion* (Handley 2017) is a brief exploration of the implications of this simple poem for contemporary life.

Chapter Three. A Rational Faith

1. This claim was once made by Elaine Cannon in 1978 while serving as president of the Young Women. President Spencer W. Kimball, then the prophet of the LDS Church, asked her to refrain from such phrasing in the future, lest it imply that members are not free to wrestle with statements made by church leaders on their own. For more elaboration on this principle in Latter-day Saint experience, see chapter 6 of *The Crucible of Doubt* by Terryl and Fiona Givens.

2. Charles Briggs, quoted in Hutchison (1992), articulated similar concepts in the late nineteenth century. He said, for example, "God had refrained from presenting in the Bible a complete system of theology, and had instead arranged that the church in each era should have only so much of the truth as it needs. Correspondingly, God had decided, for the purpose of revelation, to make use of the various languages of humanity instead of creating a 'holy language'" (92). Augustus Strong similarly wrestled with the paradox of belief in transcendent revealed truth and the fact of the historicism of human language and cultures. See Grant Wacker's *Augustus Strong and the Dilemma of Historical Consciousness* (2018). Hans-Georg Gadamer would argue after Bennion that human understanding is always embedded in cultural biases and contexts but can therefore be the catalyst for insight. For an examination of Gadamer's relevance to Latter-day Saint theology, see Terryl Givens's "Poetics of Prejudice" (2017).

3. As John Durham Peters (2019) says in his insightful essay about Tara Westover's *Educated*, "Few religions are as obsessively invested in education" as Mormonism. Peters argues that Latter-day Saints have used higher education, to an unusual degree, to facilitate their transition from provinciality and isolation to global citizenship. Bennion was, in other words, not unusual in his emphasis on education but did stand out in his particular vision of how

members could navigate the waters of that transition while keeping their religious loyalty intact.

4. For a survey of attitudes of young Mormons, see Jana Riess's *Next Mormons* (2019).

5. On questions pertaining to fallibility and institutional error, see Patrick Mason's *Planted: Belief and Belonging in an Age of Doubt (2015).*

6. He said, "A friend of mine observed, 'The LDS church suffers as much from its uncritical lovers as from its unloving critics. What it needs more of is loving critics.' I agree" (1988a, vi).

7. Currently, Gospel Topics essays has fourteen essays on controversial or difficult topics related to LDS doctrine and history, including the priesthood ban. They can be accessed at *Gospel Topics Essays*, https://www.churchofjesuschrist.org/study/manual/gospel-topics-essays/essays?lang=eng.

Chapter Four. Social Morality

1. Thurman's most significant work in this regard was *Jesus and the Disinherited* from 1949 (Thurman 1996), a profound reorientation of Christian theology toward the victims of injustice.

2. Bennion appears to have followed this theological school throughout his life, as is evident in his citation of *The Social Teaching of the Christian Churches* by Ernst Troeltsch (2009). Troeltsch was a contemporary of Max Weber who detailed the many ways Christian churches had had to accommodate or rebel against prevailing social conditions of their societies.

3. Other verses he was fond of quoting with a similar message are Amos 5:21–24, Isaiah 1:11–17, and Jeremiah 7:2–7.

4. Thirty thousand was Bennion's own estimate. It would require a second book to give proper account of the influence this had on a generation of the LDS Church. Thousands of individuals were changed by Bennion's example and the direct opportunities of service he provided, inspiring them to shape their various careers and life paths according to the principles of social morality.

5. Latter-day Saints business thought leaders and practitioners today enjoy a significant influence in business, but their influence is more notable in the realm of personal ethics than in social morality. One enormously popular and almost universally admired Latter-day Saint business scholar is Clayton Christensen. His 2012 book, *How Will You Measure Your Life?*, elaborates the moral principles of a value-driven life in inspiring ways, but it says less about why to use a career for social good or about how to invest or spend one's income, questions that preoccupied Bennion. *The Mormon Way of Doing Business: Leadership and Success through Faith and Family* by Jeff Benedict (2007) similarly highlights the personal habits and family commitments of LDS businessmen

but does not explore what Mormonism implies about how or why to leverage a career for improvement of the underprivileged or any specifics about the appropriate level of consumption at which one should live.

6. For a biography and analysis of Young's social morality, see John G. Turner's 2014 book, *Brigham Young: Pioneer Prophet*.

7. On this point, see Ezra Klein (2021) and Bill Bishop (2008).

8. See, for example, Lilliana Mason (2018).

9. Bennion was even more specific. He was not afraid to identify a reasonable price for a home, beyond which one might create moral risk. "If a home is sturdy, comfortable, sufficiently roomy for a family's needs, and aesthetically pleasing, then that home is adequate. I realize that housing is very expensive but such a home as I describe, suitable for an average family, can easily be found in Salt Lake City for $60,000 to $150,000 (at least in the late 1980s)" (1988a, 44). It is perhaps a tragic irony that a housing shortage has caused prices in Salt Lake City to climb much more dramatically in recent decades and have steadily outpaced average income. The median house price in 2022 in many ZIP codes in the Salt Lake area is over $800,000, a price that will likely sound modest in the decades to come.

10. For a thorough reading of the Book of Mormon's condemnation of excessive wealth and persecution of the poor and its relevance to US culture today, see Kristin Matthews (2015).

11. The most significant work on race and racism in the LDS Church of Jesus Christ of Latter-day Saints is provided by Paul Reeve (2017). Reeve's study paints a picture of the long historical struggle over race that was central to the Mormon experience, and it offers a context to appreciate the significance of Bennion's long-standing challenging but faithful dialogue with the LDS Church over the priesthood ban. Another study by Joanna Brooks (2020) focuses more on the activism and treatment of famous dissenters. Brooks neglects to mention Bennion, who was longer in the struggle and had arguably more influence than the more public opponents of the LDS Church's policy, especially in the strong ethical underpinnings he identified in LDS theology and offered for future generations in his teaching and writing.

12. For an elaboration on Benson's reading of the Book of Mormon, see Harris (2020).

13. For one LDS example, see Richard Williams, "America's Impending Acid Test" (2020).

Notes to Chapter Four

Works Cited

Allen, James. 2019. *As a Man Thinketh.* Shippensburg, PA: Sound Wisdom.

Arendt, Hannah. 2006. *Eichmann in Jerusalem: A Report on the Banality of Evil.* New York: Viking Penguin.

Benedict, Jeff. 2007. *The Mormon Way of Doing Business: Leadership and Success through Faith and Family.* New York: Business Plus.

Bennion, Lowell L. 1933. *Max Weber's Methodology.* Paris: Presses Modernes.

———. 1940. *The Religion of the Latter-day Saints.* Salt Lake City: L.D.S. Department of Education.

———. 1955. *An Introduction to the Gospel.* Salt Lake City: Deseret Sunday School Union Board.

———. 1959. *Religion and the Pursuit of Truth.* Salt Lake City: Deseret Book.

———. 1978. *The Things That Matter Most.* Salt Lake City: Bookcraft.

———. 1981. *Jesus the Master Teacher.* Salt Lake City: Deseret Book.

———. 1983. *I Believe.* Salt Lake City: Deseret Book.

———. 1985a. *The Book of Mormon: A Guide to Christian Living.* Salt Lake City: Desert Book.

———. 1985b. "Lowell L. Bennion Oral History." Interview by Maureen Ursenbach Beecher, January 26. Salt Lake City: Church of Jesus Christ of Latter-day Saints History Department.

———. 1985c. "Saint for All Seasons: An Interview with Lowell L. Bennion." *Sunstone* 10, no. 2: 1–17.

———. 1988a. *Do Justly and Love Mercy: Moral Issues for Mormons.* Centerville, UT: Canon.

———. 1988b. *The Unknown Testament.* Salt Lake City: Deseret Book.

———. 1990. *Legacies of Jesus.* Salt Lake City: Deseret Book.

———. 1996. *How Can I Help? Final Selections by the Legendary Writer, Teacher, and Humanitarian.* Murray, UT: Aspen.

Bennion, Milton. 1919. *Citizenship: An Introduction to Social Ethics*. New York: World Book.

———. 1928. *Moral Teachings of the New Testament*. Salt Lake City: Deseret Book.

Benson, Ezra Taft. 1989. "Born of God." https://www.churchofjesuschrist.org/study/ensign/1989/07/born-of-god?lang=eng.

Berry, Wendell. 2010. *What Are People For?* Berkeley, CA: Counterpoint.

Bishop, Bill. 2008. *The Big Sort: Why the Clustering of Like-Minded America Is Tearing Us Apart*. New York: Houghton Mifflin Harcourt.

Blakely, Thomas. 1986. "The Swearing Elders: The First Generation of Modern Mormon Intellectuals." *Sunstone* 10: 8–13.

Bowman, Matthew. 2012. *The Mormon People: The Making of an American Faith*. New York: Random House.

Bradford, Mary Lythgoe. 1995. *Lowell L. Bennion: Teacher, Counselor, Humanitarian*. Salt Lake City: Dialogue Foundation.

Brooks, Joanna. 2020. *Mormonism and White Supremacy: American Religion and the Problem of White Innocence*. Oxford: Oxford University Press.

Buber, Martin. 1972. *I and Thou*. Translated by Walter Kaufmann. New York: Scribner's.

Christensen, Clayton M., James Allsworth, and Karen Dillon. 2012. *How Will You Measure Your Life?* New York: Harper Business.

Clark, J. Reuben Jr. 1938. *The Charted Course of the Church in Education*. Salt Lake City: Church of Jesus Christ of Latter-day Saints. https://www.churchofjesuschrist.org/bc/content/shared/content/english/pdf/language-materials/32709_eng.pdf?lang=eng.

England, Eugene, ed. 1988. *The Best of Lowell L. Bennion: Selected Writings 1928–1988*. Salt Lake City: Deseret Book.

England, Eugene. 1996. "The Legacy of Lowell L. Bennion." *Sunstone* 19, no. 3: 27–44.

Esplin, Scott C. 2006. "Charting the Course: President Clark's Charge to Religious Educators." *Religious Educator* 7, no. 1: 103–19. https://rsc.byu.edu/vol-7-no-1-2006/charting-course-president-clarks-charge-religious-educators.

Fosdick, Harry Emerson. 1943. *On Being a Real Person*. New York: HarperCollins.

Givens, Terryl. 2017. "Poetics of Prejudice." In *To Be Learned Is Good: Essays on Faith and Scholarship in Honor of Richard Lyman Bushman*. Edited by Spencer Fluhman, Kathleen Flake, and Jed Woodworth, 21–33. Provo, UT: Neal A. Maxwell Institute for Religious Scholarship.

———. 2021. *Stretching the Heavens: The Life of Eugene England and the Crisis of Modern Mormonism*. Chapel Hill: University of North Carolina Press.

Givens, Terryl, and Fiona Givens. 2014. *The Crucible of Doubt: Reflections on the Quest for Faith*. Salt Lake City: Deseret Book.

Goldberg, Robert Alan, L. Jackson Newell, and Linda King Newell. 2018. *Conscience and Community: Sterling McMurrin, Obert C. Tanner, and Lowell L. Bennion*. Salt Lake City: University of Utah Press.

Gospel Topics Essays. 2022. https://www.churchofjesuschrist.org/study/manual /gospel-topics-essays/essays?lang=eng.

Handley, George B. 2017. *Learning to Like Life: A Tribute to Lowell Bennion*. CreateSpace Platform.

Harris, Matthew. 2020. *Watchman on the Tower: Ezra Taft Benson and the Making of the Mormon Right*. Salt Lake City: University of Utah Press.

Hinckley, Gordon B. 2006. "President Hinckley on Racial Intolerance." Priesthood session, April 2006 General Conference. https://newsroom.church ofjesuschrist.org/ldsnewsroom/eng/background-information/president -gordon-b-hinckley-on-racial-intolerance.

Hutchison, William R. 1992. *The Modernist Impulse in American Protestantism*. Durham, NC: Duke University Press.

Jacobs, Alan. 2001. *A Theology of Reading: A Hermeneutics of Love*. Abingdon, UK: Routledge.

Jesuits. 2022. https://www.jesuits.org/.

Keating, Thomas. 1992. *Invitation to Love*. New York: Bloomsbury.

Klein, Ezra. 2021. *Why We're Polarized*. New York: Simon and Schuster.

Maslow, Abraham. 1954. *Motivation and Personality*. New York: Harper and Brothers.

Mason, Lilliana. 2018. *Uncivil Agreement: How Politics Became Our Identity*. Chicago: University of Chicago Press.

Mason, Patrick. 2015. Planted: Belief and Belonging in an Age of Doubt. Salt Lake City: Deseret Book

Matthews, Kristin. 2015. "'Come into the Fold of God': Caring for the Poor and Needy." Laura F. Willes Book of Mormon Lecture. Neal A. Maxwell Institute for Religious Scholarship, Brigham Young University, Provo, UT. https:// www.youtube.com/watch?v=7V71hwNm_DM.

McBaine, Neylan. 2014. *Women at Church: Magnifying LDS Women's Local Impact*. Salt Lake City: Greg Kofford.

Miller, Adam S. 2018a. *An Early Resurrection: Life in Christ before You Die*. Salt Lake City: Deseret Book.

———. 2018b. *Letters to a Young Mormon*. Salt Lake City: Deseret Book.

O'Dea, Thomas. 1957. *The Mormons*. Chicago: University of Chicago Press.

Packer, Boyd K. 1986. "Little Children." October 1986 General Conference. https://www.churchofjesuschrist.org/study/general-conference/1986/10 /little-children?lang=eng.

Peters, John Durham. 2019. "Another Mormon Education." *Public Books*, July 30. https://www.publicbooks.org/another-mormon-education/.

Phillips, J. B. 2004. *Your God Is Too Small: A Guide for Believers and Skeptics Alike*. New York: Touchstone.

Quinn, D. Michael. 2002. Elder Stateman: A Biography of J. Reuben Clark. Salt Lake City: Signature.

Rauschenbusch, Walter. 2008. *Christianity and the Social Crisis: The Classic That Woke Up the Church*. New York: HarperOne. Kindle edition.

Reeve, W. Paul. 2017. *Religion of a Different Color: Race and the Mormon Struggle for Whiteness*. Oxford: Oxford University Press.

Ricoeur, Paul. 1980. *Essays on Biblical Interpretation*. New York: Fortress.

Riess, Jana. 2019. *The Next Mormons: How Millennials Are Changing the LDS Church*. Oxford: Oxford University Press.

Sachs, Jeffrey. 2006. *The End of Poverty: Economic Possibilities for Our Time*. New York: Penguin.

Schweitzer, Albert. 2014. *Out of My Life and Thought: An Autobiography*. Translated by A. B. Lemke. New York: Henry Holt.

Simpson, Thomas W. 2016. *American Universities and the Birth of Modern Mormonism, 1867–1940*. Chapel Hill: University of North Carolina Press.

Taylor, Charles. 2007. *A Secular Age*. Cambridge, MA: Belnap.

Thurman, Howard. 1996. *Jesus and the Disinherited*. Boston: Beacon Press.

Torrey, R. A., and A. C. Dixon. 1972. *The Fundamentals: A Testimony to the Truth*. 4 vols. Grand Rapids, MI: Baker. Reprint of 1917.

Troeltsch, Ernst. 2009. *The Social Teachings of the Christian Churches*. Louisville, KY: Westminster John Knox Press.

Turner, John G. 2014. *Brigham Young: Pioneer Prophet*. Cambridge, MA: Belknap.

Utah Food Bank. 2022. https://www.utahfoodbank.org/about/history/#:~:text=Utah%20Food%20Bank%20was%20founded,agencies%20in%20Salt%20Lake%20City.

Wacker, Grant. 2018. *Augustus H. Strong and the Dilemma of Historical Consciousness*. Waco, TX: Baylor University Press.

Weber, Max. 1949. "Objectivity in Social Science and Social Policy" in *The Methodology of the Social Sciences*. Translated and edited by E. A. Shils and H. A. Finch. New York: Free Press.

Williams, Richard. 2020. "America's Impending Acid Test." Public Square. https://publicsquaremag.org/dialogue/americas-impending-acid-test/.

Index

abortion, 83, 107–8
Allen, James, 33, 47
Alma, teachings of, 60, 62–63, 90, 95, 99.
  See also Book of Mormon
As a Man Thinketh, 33, 47

Barlow, Philip, 3
Beeley, Arthur, 9, 13
Bennion, Ben (Lowell C.), 18
Bennion, Cora, 8
Bennion, Doug, 18
Bennion, Ellen, 18
Bennion, Howard, 18–19
Bennion, Laurel Colton, 12
Bennion, Lowell L.: awards of, 79; character
  of, 18, 26; childhood of, 8–9; death of, 26;
  education of, 9, 10, 12; marriage of, 9–10;
  early work of, 12–13; family life/parent-
  hood of, 12, 18–19; popularity decline, 3, 7,
  14, 25–26; tension with church institution,
  5, 7, 51–52, 74, 101–4
Bennion Lowell L., books by. See *Book of
  Mormon: Guide to Christian Living*; *Do
  Justly and Love Mercy: Moral Issues for
  Mormons*; *How Can I Help?*; *I Believe*;
  Introduction to the Gospel; *Jesus the Mas-
  ter Teacher*; *Legacies of Jesus*; *Max Weber's
  Methodology*; *Religion and the Pursuit of
  Truth*; *Religion of the Latter-day Saints*;
  Selected Wisdom from World Religions;
  Things that Matter Most; *Unknown Testa-
  ment*
Bennion, Lowell, L., essays by: "Church
  and the Larger Society," 106; "For By

Grace Are Ye Saved," 106; "Overcoming
  Prejudice," 106; "What It Means to Be a
  Latter-day Saint," 106
Bennion, Merle. *See* Colton, Merle
Bennion, Milton, 8–9, 12, 78
Bennion, M. Lynn, 6
Bennion, Steve, 18
Benson, Ezra Taft, 16, 46–47, 99
Berry, Wendel, 93
Best of Lowell Bennion, The, 105. *See also*
  England, Eugene
Book of Mormon: Bennion's approach to,
  66, 92, 110; and race, 99–100; teachings
  of, 62, 63, 66, 95. *See also* Alma, teach-
  ings of; *Book of Mormon: Guide to Chris-
  tian Living*
Book of Mormon: Guide to Christian Living
  (Bennion, 1985), 40, 50, 53, 80, 84, 99;
  race, teachings about, 98–100; revelation,
  teachings about, 58–60, 62–63, 66, 70;
  service, teachings about, 82, 87, 90; social
  morality, 80, 85, 90, 93, 95. *See also* Book
  of Mormon
Book of Moses, 39. *See also* Smith, Joseph
Bowman, Matthew, 15, 35
Boyd, George, 16
boys' ranch, 1, 24–25, 46–47
Bradford, Mary, 24
Briggs, Charles, 28, 29, 114n2
Brigham Young University, 4, 15–16, 20,
  23, 73. *See also* Church Education Sys-
  tem
Browne, Borden Parker, 33
Buber, Martin, 33, 113n1 (ch. 2)

Cannon, Elaine, 114n1

capitalism, 10–11, 45, 92–94, 101–2. *See also* communism

Charted Course of the Church in Education, The, 6, 13–14, 73–74. *See also* Clark, J. Reuben

Chase, Daryl, 16

Christensen, Clayton, 115n5 (ch. 4)

Christianity and the Social Crisis, 15–16, 82. *See also* Rauschenbusch, Walter

Church Education System, 20, 23, 73–75. *See also* Brigham Young University; Church of Jesus Christ of Latter-day Saints, and education; Wilkinson, Ernest

Church of Jesus Christ of Latter-day Saints: and education, 30, 51, 64–65, 73–75, 114n3 (ch. 3); correlation of materials, 4, 26, 64–65; history of, 41; as an international church, 4, 26; and politics, 4, 50, 88, 94, 102–3; and race, 7–8, 27, 88, 89, 116n11; theology of, 44–45, 60, 81. *See also* Church Education System; Gospel Topics essays

civil rights, 7, 28, 83, 88, 107. *See also* racism; Thurman, Howard

Clark, J. Reuben, 13–15, 80; *The Charted Course of the Church in Education,* 6, 13–14, 73–74

Coe, George, 28

Colton, Merle, 9–10, 12–13, 18–19

communism, 23, 45–46, 81, 93, 101–2. *See also* capitalism; Church of Jesus Christ of Latter-day Saints, and politics

Community Services Council, Salt Lake City, 25

Cowley, Matthew, 41

Deseret Book, 9, 25, 105

Dialogue, 19, 25, 64, 105

Doctrine and Covenants, 44–45, 50, 59. *See also* Smith, Joseph

Do Justly and Love Mercy: Moral Issues for Mormons (Bennion, 1988), 61, 77, 80, 92, 107; abortion, teachings about, 108; morals, teaching about, 44, 51, 92; politics and economics, 83–84, 93–98, 101–3, 116n9; social morality, teachings about, 80, 81–82, 85–86, 97, 107; thinking critically about religion, 71, 72, 115n6

England, Eugene, 3, 64, 106, 113n3; *The Best of Lowell Bennion,* 105

ethical monotheism, 80, 91

Faust, 67

Fosdick, Harry Emerson, 33–34

Fundamentals, The, 15

Gadamer, Hans-Georg, 114n2

General Conference, Bennion's addresses in, 2, 20, 31, 106

Givens, Terryl, 14

Goethe, 67

Gospel Topics essays, 8, 76, 115n7 (ch. 3). *See also* racism

Graham, Billy, 46

Grant, Heber J., 81

Hinckley, Gordon B., 7–8, 26

Hitler, Adolf, 12. *See also* Nazism

homosexuality, 18, 102–3, 108–9

How Can I Help? (Bennion, 1996), 3, 38, 41–43, 44, 48–51, 85–87, 105; social justice, teachings about, 88, 89; women, teachings to, 107

I and Thou, 33, 113n1 (ch. 2)

I Believe (Bennion, 1983), 2, 49–50, 66, 81, 110–12; Bennion's personal testimony, 38, 58, 111–12; grace, teachings about, 86; relationships with other people, teachings about, 38, 39, 86, 101; sin, teachings about, 39, 40–41

Introduction to the Gospel, An, (Bennion, 1955), 23, 55–56; teachings of, 65, 69, 71

Jacobs, Alan, 61

Jesuits, 28

Jesus the Master Teacher (Bennion, 1981), 41, 42

Keating, Thomas, 40

Kimball, Spencer W., 7, 114n1

King, Henry Churchill, 28

Legacies of Jesus (Bennion, 1990), 22, 39

LGBT rights, 102. *See also* homosexuality

Lotze, Hermann, 28

Lyon, T. Edgar, 13, 16, 17, 19

Marxism, 10. *See also* communism

Maslow, Abraham, 35, 42–43

materialism, 43–44, 49–50, 92–92. *See also* capitalism

Max Weber's Methodology (Bennion, 1933) 10–12, 34–35. *See also* Weber, Max

McBaine, Neylan, 107

McKay, David O.: presidency of, 20, 45; relationship with Bennion, 13, 19, 21, 24, 58; and temple/priesthood ban, 5, 20–21, 58
McMurrin, Sterling, 16, 19, 29
Mormon History Association, 19
Mormonism. *See* Church of Jesus Christ of Latter-day Saints
Mormon renaissance, 9, 12, 26
Mormon Seminar, 19, 64
Mormons, The, 2–3, 15, 30, 103–4. *See also* O'Dea, Thomas
Mormon Studies, 19
Morris, William, 33
Munger, Theodore, 28

Nazism, 10, 45–46, 57
Nelson, Russell M., 8
New Deal, 81
New Thought, 33–34, 44
Nibley, Hugh, 3, 92

O'Dea, Thomas, 2–4, 75; *The Mormons*, 2–3, 15, 30, 103–4
On Being a Real Person, 33–34.

Packer, Boyd K., 74–75
Peterson, Mark E., 20–21
Phillips, J. B., 55
politics, 83–84, 101–3: Bennion's ideologies, 62, 81, 102; increasing political polarization, 8, 30; and religion, 32, 52, 93–94. *See also* Church of Jesus Christ of Latter-day Saints; communism
priesthood ban, 7–8, 20–21, 23; compared to opposition to gay marriage, 108; justifications for, 8, 22, 61; reversal of, 7, 27; seen as incompatible with the gospel, 5, 61, 76–77, 98, 113n3. *See also* McKay, David O.; racism

racism, 7–8, 27, 76–77, 89, 98–101. *See also* Book of Mormon, and race; civil rights; priesthood ban
Rauschenbusch, Walter, 15, 28; *Christianity and the Social Crisis*, 15–16, 82
Reeve, Paul, 116n11
Religion and the Pursuit of Truth (Bennion, 1959), 23, 109; teachings of, 48–49, 51–53, 55–62, 65–72, 75

Religion of the Latter-day Saints, The (Bennion, 1940), 3, 6, 13, 39, 42, 55, 66–67, 71; agency, teaching about, 45; humans as intelligences, 42, 44; as response to J. Rueben Clark, 6, 13. *See also Charted Course of the Church in Education*
Ricoeur, Paul, 61
Ritschl, Albrecht, 28
Roberts, B. H., 16, 35
Roosevelt, Franklin, 81

Sachs, Jeffery, 93
Schweitzer, Albert, 12, 78–79, 82, 85, 107–8
Selected Wisdom from World Religions (Bennion, n.d.), 105
Smith, Joseph, 20, 21, 29, 44, 60, 73
Smith, Joseph Fielding, 16, 20–22, 113n4
Sperry, Sydney, 15
Strong, Augustus, 114n2
Sunstone, 19, 25, 64, 105
Swearing Elders, 19, 64
Swensen, Russel, 16

Talmage, James, 16, 35
Tanner, Obert C., 19, 29
temple ban. *See* priesthood ban
Things that Matter Most, The (Bennion, 1978), 36, 105; teachings of, 36–39, 45
Thurman, Howard, 80, 115n1. *See also* civil rights
Troeltch, Ernst, 115n2

Unknown Testament, The (Bennion, 1988), 80; teachings of, 80, 81–82, 86, 88–91
Utah Food Bank, 25

Weber, Max, 10–11, 28; Weberian ideas, 22, 34–35, 41, 68, 91. *See also Max Weber's Methodology*
West, Frank, 16
Westover, Tara, 114n3 (ch. 3)
Widstoe, John, 5–6, 12–13, 16, 35
Wilkinson, Ernest, 16, 20, 23–24
women's rights, 8, 106–7, 113n2 (ch. 2)

Young, Brigham, 13, 60, 66, 92–93; and education, 13, 73; and priesthood ban, 7, 20

GEORGE B. HANDLEY is a professor
of interdisciplinary humanities at Brigham
Young University. His books include *The Hope
of Nature: Our Care for God's Creation.*

Introductions to Mormon Thought

Eugene England: A Mormon Liberal   *Kristine L. Haglund*
Vardis Fisher: A Mormon Novelist   *Michael Austin*
Lowell L. Bennion: A Mormon Educator   *George B. Handley*

The University of Illinois Press
is a founding member of the
Association of University Presses.

Composed in 10.75/14 Adobe Minion Pro
with DIN display
by Kirsten Dennison
at the University of Illinois Press
Manufactured by Sheridan Books, Inc.

University of Illinois Press
1325 South Oak Street
Champaign, IL 61820-6903
www.press.uillinois.edu